# AAT

## INTERACTIVE TEXT

Foundation Unit 3

# Ledger Balances and Initial Trial Balance

**In this May 2001 edition**

- Layout designed to be easier on the eye - and easy to use
- Icons to guide you through a 'fast track' approach if you wish
- Numerous activities throughout the text to reinforce learning
- Thorough reliable updating of material to 1 May 2001

**FOR 2001 AND 2002 ASSESSMENTS**

**BPP Publishing**
*May 2001*

*First edition 2000*
*Second edition May 2001*

*ISBN 0 7517 6504 X (Previous edition 0 7517 6207 5)*

***British Library Cataloguing-in-Publication Data***
*A catalogue record for this book*
*is available from the British Library*

*Published by*

*BPP Publishing Limited*
*Aldine House, Aldine Place*
*London W12 8AW*

*www.bpp.com*

*Printed in Great Britain by W M Print*
*45-47 Frederick Street*
*Walsall*
*West Midlands*
*WS2 9NE*



*We are also grateful to the Lead Body for Accounting for permission to reproduce extracts from the Standards of Competence for Accounting, and to the AAT for permission to reproduce extracts from the mapping and Guidance Notes.*

# HOW TO USE THIS INTERACTIVE TEXT

## Aims of this Interactive Text

To provide the knowledge and practice to help you succeed in the central and devolved assessments for Foundation Unit 3 *Preparing Ledger Balances and an Initial Trial Balance.*

To pass the assessments you need a thorough understanding in all areas covered by the standards of competence.

To tie in with the other components of the BPP Effective Study Package to ensure you have the best possible chance of success.

**Interactive Text**
This covers all you need to know for the central and devolved assessments for Unit 3 *Preparing Ledger Balances and an Initial Trial Balance.* Icons clearly mark key areas of the text. Numerous activities throughout the text help you practise what you have just learnt.

**Central and Devolved Assessment Kit**
When you have understood and practised the material in the Interactive Text, you will have the knowledge and experience to tackle the Central and Devolved Assessment Kit for Unit 3 *Preparing Ledger Balances and an Initial Trial Balance*. This aims to get you through the central assessment and the devolved assessment, whether in the form of the AAT simulation or in the workplace.

## Recommended approach to this Interactive Text

(a) To achieve competence in Unit 3 (and all the other units), you need to be able to do **everything** specified by the standards. Study the Interactive Text carefully and do not skip any of it.

(b) Learning is an **active** process. Do **all** the activities as you work through the Interactive Text so you can be sure you really understand what you have read.

(c) After you have covered the material in the Interactive Text, work through the **Assessment Kit**.

(d) Before you take the assessments, check that you still remember the material using the following quick revision plan for each chapter.

   (i) Read through the chapter learning objectives. Are there any gaps in your knowledge? If so, study the section again.

   (ii) Read and learn the key terms.

   (iii) Look at the assessment alerts. These show the sort of things that are likely to come up.

   (iv) Read and learn the key learning points, which are a summary of the chapter.

   (v) Do the quick quiz again. If you know what you're doing, it shouldn't take long.

   This approach is only a suggestion. Your college may well adapt it to suit your needs.

Remember this is a **practical** course.

(a) Try to relate the material to your experience in the workplace or any other work experience you may have had.

(b) Try to make as many links as you can to your study of the other Units at Foundation level.

(c) Keep this text, (hopefully) you will find it invaluable in your everyday work too!

## FOUNDATION QUALIFICATION STRUCTURE

The competence-based Education and Training Scheme of the Association of Accounting Technicians is based on an analysis of the work of accounting staff in a wide range of industries and types of organisation. The Standards of Competence for Accounting which students are expected to meet are based on this analysis.

The Standards identify the key purpose of the accounting occupation, which is to operate, maintain and improve systems to record, plan, monitor and report on the financial activities of an organisation, and a number of key roles of the occupation. Each key role is subdivided into units of competence, which are further divided into elements of competences. By successfully completing assessments in specified units of competence, students can gain qualifications at NVQ/SVQ levels 2, 3 and 4, which correspond to the AAT Foundation, Intermediate and Technician stages of competence respectively.

Whether you are competent in a Unit is demonstrated by means of:

- *Either* a Central Assessment (set and marked by AAT assessors)
- *Or* a Devolved Assessment (where competence is judged by an Approved Assessment Centre to whom responsibility for this is devolved)
- Or *both* Central *and* Devolved Assessment

Below we set out the overall structure of the Foundation (NVQ/SVQ Level 2) stage, indicating how competence in each Unit is assessed. In the next section there is more detail about the Devolved Assessment for Unit 3.

All units are assessed by Devolved Assessment, and Unit 3 is also assessed by Central Assessment.

## NVQ/SVQ Level 2 - Foundation (All units are mandatory)

| Unit of competence | | Elements of competence | |
|---|---|---|---|
| Unit 1 | Recording income and receipts | 1.1 | Process documents relating to goods and services supplied |
| | | 1.2 | Receive and record receipts |
| Unit 2 | Making and recording payments | 2.1 | Process documents relating to goods and services received |
| | | 2.2 | Prepare authorised payments |
| | | 2.3 | Make and record payments |
| Unit 3 | Preparing ledger balances and an initial trial balance | 3.1 | Balance bank transactions |
| | | 3.2 | Prepare ledger balances and control accounts |
| | | 3.3 | Draft an initial trial balance |
| Unit 4 | Supplying information for management control | 4.1 | Code and extract information |
| | | 4.2 | Provide comparisons on costs and income |
| Unit 20 | Working with information technology | 20.1 | Input, store and output data |
| | | 20.2 | Minimise risks to data held on a computer system |
| Unit 22 | Monitor and maintain a healthy safe and secure workplace (ASC) | 22.1 | Monitor and maintain health and safety within the workplace |
| | | 22.2 | Monitor and maintain the security of the workplace |
| Unit 23 | Achieving personal effectiveness | 23.1 | Plan and organise own work |
| | | 23.2 | Establish and maintain working relationships |
| | | 23.3 | Maintain accounting files and records |

# UNIT 3 STANDARDS OF COMPETENCE

## The structure of the Standards for Unit 3

The Unit commences with a statement of the **knowledge and understanding** which underpin competence in the Unit's elements.

The Unit of Competence is then divided into **elements of competence** describing activities which the individual should be able to perform.

Each element includes:

(a) **A** set of **performance criteria.** This defines what constitutes competent performance.

(b) A **range statement.** This defines the situations, contexts, methods etc in which competence should be displayed.

(c) **Evidence requirements.** These state that competence must be demonstrated consistently, over an appropriate time scale with evidence of performance being provided from the appropriate sources.

(d) **Sources of evidence.** These are suggestions of ways in which you can find evidence to demonstrate that competence. These fall under the headings: 'observed performance; work produced by the candidate; authenticated testimonies from relevant witnesses; personal account of competence; other sources of evidence.' They are reproduced in full in our Assessment Kit for Unit 3.

The elements of competence for Unit 3 *Preparing Ledger Balances and an Initial Trial Balance* are set out below. Knowledge and understanding required for the unit as a whole are listed first, followed by the performance criteria and range statements for each element. Performance criteria are cross-referenced below to chapters in this Unit 3 *Ledger Balances and Initial Trial Balance* Interactive Text.

## Unit 3: Preparing Ledger Balances and an Initial Trial Balance

*What is the unit about?*

This unit relates to the internal checks involved in an organisation's accounting processes. The first element is primarily concerned with comparing individual items on the bank statement with entries in the cash book, and identifying any discrepancies. This involves recording details from the relevant primary documentation, including cheque counterfoils, paying-in slips and standing order schedules, in the cash book, and calculating the totals and balances of receipts and payments. The element also requires the individual to identify any discrepancies, such as uncertainty in coding and differences identified by the matching process.

The second element requires the individual to total the relevant accounts and to reconcile the control accounts, such as debtors, creditors, cash and wages and salaries, with the totals of the balance in the ledgers. The individual is also required to resolve or refer any discrepancies and to ensure security and confidentiality.

The third element involves identifying and obtaining the information required for an initial trial balance from the computer system, relevant files, ledgers, colleagues and the appropriate managers and accountants. The element requires the individual to prepare the trial balance in the appropriate format up to the draft stage, seeking advice from the relevant people where necessary.

## Knowledge and understanding

**The business environment**

- Types of business transactions and the documents involved (Elements 3.1 & 3.2)
- General bank services and operation of bank clearing system (Element 3.1)
- Function and form of banking documentation (Element 3.1)

**Accounting methods**

- Operation of manual and computerised accounting systems (Elements 3.1, 3.2 & 3.3)
- Identification of different types of errors (Element 3.1)
- Relationship between the accounting system and the ledger (Elements 3.1 & 3.2)
- Methods of posting from primary records to ledger accounts (Element 3.2)
- Inter-relationship of accounts - double entry system (Elements 3.2 & 3.3)
- Use of journals (Elements 3.2 & 3.3)
- Methods of closing off ledger accounts (Element 3.2)
- Reconciling control accounts with memorandum accounts (Element 3.2)
- Function and form of the trial balance (Element 3.3)

**The organisation**

- Relevant understanding of the organisation's accounting systems and administrative systems and procedures (Elements 3.1, 3.2 & 3.3)
- The nature of the organisation's business transactions (Elements 3.1, 3.2 & 3.3)
- Organisational procedures for filing source information (Elements 3.1, 3.2 & 3.3)

## Element 3.1 Balance bank transactions

| | Performance criteria | Chapters in this Text |
|---|---|---|
| 1 | Details from the relevant primary documentation are recorded in the cash book | 1, 2 |
| 2 | Totals and balances of receipts and payments are correctly calculated | 1, 2 |
| 3 | Individual items on the bank statement and in the cash book are compared for accuracy | 4 |
| 4 | Discrepancies are identified and referred to the appropriate person | 1 - 8 |

**Range statement**

1. Primary documentation: credit transfer and standing order schedules
2. Discrepancies: uncertainty in coding; differences identified by the matching process

## Element 3.2 Prepare ledger balances and control accounts

| Performance criteria | | Chapters in this Text |
|---|---|---|
| 1 | Relevant accounts are totalled | 1, 2 |
| 2 | Control accounts are reconciled with the totals of the balance in the subsidiary ledger, where appropriate | 6, 7 |
| 3 | Authorised adjustments are correctly processed and documented | 1 - 7 |
| 4 | Discrepancies arising from the reconciliation of control accounts are either resolved or referred to the appropriate person | 6, 7 |
| 5 | Documentation is stored securely and in line with the organisation's confidentiality requirements | 8 |

**Range statement**

1 Ledgers: main ledger; sub ledger; integrated ledger

2 Control accounts: stock; debtors; creditors; cash; wages and salaries

3 Adjustments: to correct errors; to write off bad debts

## Element 3.3 Draft an initial trial balance

| Performance criteria | | Chapters in this Text |
|---|---|---|
| 1 | Information required for the initial trial balance is identified and obtained from the relevant sources | 3 |
| 2 | Relevant people are asked for advice when the necessary information is not available | 3 |
| 3 | The draft initial trial balance is prepared in line with the organisation's policies and procedures | 3 |
| 4 | Discrepancies are identified in the balancing process and referred to the appropriate person | 3 |

**Range statement**

1 Sources: colleagues; computer system; files; manager; accountant; ledger

2 Discrepancies: incorrect double entries; missing entries; wrong calculations

## ASSESSMENT STRATEGY AND GUIDANCE

This unit is assessed by **devolved assessment** and **central assessment**.

### Devolved Assessment *(More detail can be found in the Assessment Kit)*

Devolved assessment is a means of collecting evidence of your ability to carry out practical activities and to **operate effectively in the conditions of the workplace** to the standards required. Evidence may be collected at your place of work or at an Approved Assessment Centre by means of simulations of workplace activity, or by a combination of these methods.

If the Approved Assessment Centre is a **workplace** you may be observed carrying out accounting activities as part of your normal work routine. You should collect documentary evidence of the work you have done, or contributed, in an **accounting portfolio.** Evidence collected in a portfolio can be assessed in addition to observed performance or where it is not possible to assess by observation.

Where the Approved Assessment Centre is a **college or training organisation**, devolved assessment will be by means of a combination of the following.

(a) Documentary evidence of activities carried out at the workplace, collected by you in an **accounting portfolio**

(b) Realistic **simulations** of workplace activities; these simulations may take the form of case studies and in-tray exercises and involve the use of primary documents and reference sources

(c) **Projects and assignments** designed to assess the Standards of Competence

If you are unable to provide workplace evidence, you will be able to complete the assessment requirements by the alternative methods listed above.

### Central Assessment

A central assessment is a means of collecting evidence that you have the **essential knowledge and understanding** which underpins competence. It is also a means of collecting evidence across the **range of contexts** for the standards, and of your ability to **transfer skills**, knowledge and understanding to different situations. Thus, although central assessments contain practical tests linked to the performance criteria, they also focus on the underpinning knowledge and understanding. You should in addition expect each central assessment to contain tasks taken from across a broad range of the standards.

### Further guidance

The following guidance is taken from the AAT's Newsletter *Summing Up*.

The first Central Assessment for the revised Foundation Level has now been held. Candidates' performance was excellent.

One of the issues which arose was that candidates need to ensure that they have mastered the technique of balancing accounts before they undertake this Unit. There have also been queries received regarding the inclusion of law (such as contracts, offers and acceptance) in the Central Assessment. The law of contract is part of the knowledge and understanding in Units 1 and 2 (Recording Income and Receipts (RIR) and Making and Recording Payments (MRP) and as such will not be included in the Central Assessment. However candidates can expect to be assessed on business documentation as this is included in the knowledge and understanding of the first three units of the revised Foundation. Indeed, questions on this issue are included in the Specimen Central Assessment. The function and form of banking documentation is also a feature of Unit 3 and as such could be centrally assessed.

There have also been queries received regarding where specific issues are assessable in the first three units of the Standards – notably balances carried down, control accounts (including debtors control accounts) and aged debtors analysis. To clarify – balances carried down are specifically referred to in the knowledge and understanding of Unit 3 (ITB) but also implied in the knowledge and understanding of Unit 1 (RIR) and Unit 2 (MRP). Reconciling control accounts are primarily an issue included in Units 3, Preparing Ledger Balances and an Initial Trial Balance (ITB), but as Units 1 and 2 (RIR and MRP) call for entries into the ledgers, the debtors and creditors control accounts will be featured in these units. Aged debtors analysis is assessable under RIR and is specifically mentioned in the range of Element 1.1 as a source document for communicating with customers.

Centres have also asked about the inclusion of bank reconciliation statements at this Stage of the Accounting NVQ/SVQ. Bank reconciliation *statements* are not included in the revised Foundation. However, bank reconciliation *activities* are – candidates will be required to undertake the matching process and recognise the cause of the difference in the balance on the bank statement and the balance in the cash book once updated. However, the candidate will only be asked to list the differences and not to produce a bank reconciliation statement.

**Summary**

**IN**

- **Matching cash book and bank statement**
- **Debtors/creditors reconciliation**
- **Short answer questions**
- **Journal entries**
- **Completion of banking and business documentation**

**OUT**

- **Contract law** (although it could be included in a portfolio)
- **Discounts other than processing aspects,** ie transfer to cash book, although students will need to know it for Unit 2
- **General VAT principles,** although the double entry will be tested
- **Legal relationship of banker and customer**
- **Legal aspects of cheques including crossing and endorsement** although this may come up indirectly as part of banking documentation
- **Credit card procedures**. Again students may have to complete a paying-in slip as part of 'business documentation'
- **Age analysis report,** which may, however, be used in the portfolio
- **Bank reconciliation statements,** although the activity will still be featured

# Part A

## Balancing transactions

# 1 Revision of basic bookkeeping

**This chapter revises the basic bookkeeping topics covered in the Interactive Text for Unit 1 *Recording income and receipts***



## Learning objectives

On completion of this chapter you will have revised how to:

- Deal with types of business transaction and the documents involved
- Handle the basics of double entry bookkeeping
- Distinguish between capital and revenue items

## Knowledge and understanding

- Types of business transactions and the documents involved
- Inter-relationship of accounts – double entry system
- The nature of the organisation's business transactions

**ASSESSMENT ALERT**

In the Central and Devolved Assessment, the knowledge and understanding that you are revising in this chapter are vital if you are to prove yourself competent. If you read through this chapter and feel you have any doubts at all about its content, you should go back to your Unit 1 Interactive Text to resolve them.

## 1 INTRODUCTION

1.1 This chapter is quick revision of topics you have already covered in Unit 1. If you have any problems with it, look back to your earlier studies.

**ASSESSMENT ALERT**

Banking documentation and coding are covered in your Unit 1 Interactive Text. Although they are mentioned in Unit 3, they belong naturally with the Unit 1 material.

## 2 BASICS OF DOUBLE ENTRY

2.1 A business is a **separate entity** from its proprietor for accounting purposes, but not for legal purposes unless it is a limited company.

**KEY TERMS**

Businesses exist to make a **profit,** which is the excess of income over expenditure. When expenditure exceeds income, the business is running at a **loss.**

An **asset** is something valuable which a business owns or has use of.

A **liability** is something which the business owes to somebody else.

**Capital** is an investment of funds with the intention of earning a return.

2.2 The **accounting equation** provides the basis for all sets of accounts:

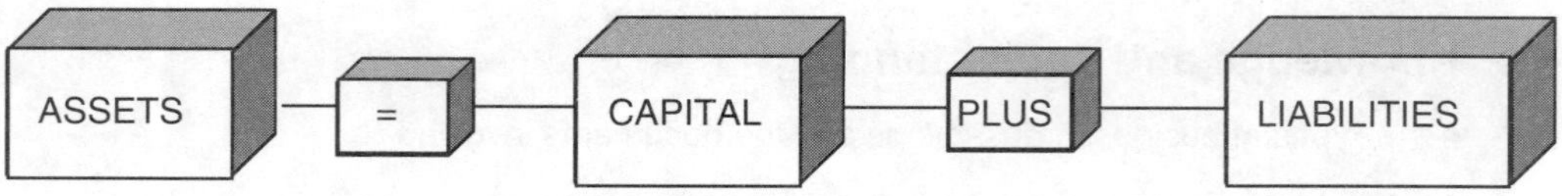


2.3 From the accounting equation we derive the basic principle of **double entry bookkeeping**.

**Every transaction gives rise to two equal accounting entries, a debit and a credit.**

2.4 The **business equation** gives a definition of profits earned within a period.

$P = I + D - C$

where:

P represents profit in the period

I represents the increase in net assets in the period, after drawings have been taken out by the proprietor

D represents drawings in the period

C represents the amount of extra capital introduced into the business during the period

**KEY TERMS**

A **cash transaction** is a sale or purchase where cash changes hands at the same time as the goods or services concerned.

A **credit transaction** is a sale or purchase which occurs some time **earlier** than cash is received or paid. It gives rise to creditors and debtors.

A **creditor** is a person from whom a business has **purchased** items and to whom a business **owes** money.

A **debtor** is a person to whom a business has **sold** items and by whom it is **owed** money.

## 3 CAPITAL AND REVENUE ITEMS

### The balance sheet

**KEY TERM**

A **balance sheet** is a statement of the assets, liabilities and capital of a business at a given moment in time.

3.1 The balance sheet is divided into two halves, showing **capital** in one half and **net assets** (assets less **liabilities**) in the other. It reflects the accounting equation, in that **one half must equal the other.**

| | |
|---|---|
| NAME OF BUSINESS | |
| BALANCE SHEET AS AT (DATE) | £ |
| Assets | X |
| Less liabilities | (X) |
| Net assets | X |
| | |
| Capital | X |

3.2 There are two types of assets.

| Fixed asset | Current asset |
|---|---|
| For use in the business not sale | Generally for use within one year |
| Make a profit over more than one accounting period | Cash or other assets (stock, debtors) which can be turned into cash within a year |

3.3 Liabilities in the balance sheet are either **current** (due to be paid within a short period, usually one year) or **long-term.**

## The profit and loss account

**KEY TERMS**

The **profit and loss account** is a statement which matches the **revenue** earned in a period with the **costs** incurred in earning it.

3.4 The profit and loss account consists of two different statements:

- The **trading account,** which shows the **gross profit**
- The **profit and loss account,** which shows the **net profit**

**Remember**

| | |
|---|---|
| Sales | X |
| Less cost of sales | (X) |
| Gross profit | X |
| Expenses | (X) |
| Net profit | X |

### Activity 1.1

(a) What is the purpose of the balance sheet?

(b) What are:

(i) Fixed assets?
(ii) Current assets?

(c) What are:

(i) Current liabilities?
(ii) Long-term liabilities?

## Capital and revenue expenditure

3.5 Some items appear in the balance sheet (**capital items**) and some appear in the profit and loss account (**revenue items**). You need to tell them apart.

**KEY TERMS**

- **Capital expenditure** is expenditure to improve or acquire fixed assets.
  - Capital expenditure on fixed assets results in the appearance of a fixed asset in the **balance sheet** of the business.
  - Capital expenditure is **not** charged as an expense in the profit and loss account.
- **Revenue expenditure** is expenditure which is incurred:

  (a) For the purpose of the trade of the business
  (b) To maintain the existing earning capacity of fixed assets

  Revenue expenditure is shown in the **profit and loss account.**
- **Capital income** is usually the proceeds from the sale of fixed assets. It is included in the **profit and loss account** of a business, for the accounting period in which the sale takes place.
- **Revenue income** is income derived from:

  (a) The sale of trading assets
  (b) Rent, interest and dividends received from fixed assets held by the business

  Revenue income appears in the profit and loss account.

## Activity 1.2

What is the difference between capital and revenue expenditure? Why is the distinction important?

## Activity 1.3

Set out below are the balance sheet and trading, profit and loss account of Spock Enterprises as at 30 April 20X7.

SPOCK ENTERPRISES
BALANCE SHEET AS AT 30 APRIL 20X7

| | £ | £ |
|---|---|---|
| *Fixed assets* | | |
| Freehold premises | | 87,500 |
| Fixtures and fittings | | 14,000 |
| Motor vehicles | | 15,750 |
| | | X |
| *Current assets* | | |
| Stocks | 28,000 | |
| Debtors | 875 | |
| Cash | 700 | |
| | X | |
| *Current liabilities* | | |
| Bank overdraft | 3,500 | |
| Creditors | 3,150 | |
| Tax payable | 6,125 | |
| | X | |
| *Net current assets* | | X |
| *Total assets less current liabilities* | | X |
| *Long-term liabilities* | | |
| Loan | | 43,750 |
| *Net assets* | | X |
| *Capital* | | |
| Capital as at 1 May 20X6 | | 76,300 |
| Profit for the year | | X |
| Capital as at 30 April 20X7 | | X |

SPOCK ENTERPRISES
TRADING, PROFIT AND LOSS ACCOUNT
FOR THE YEAR ENDED 30 APRIL 20X7

| | £ | £ |
|---|---|---|
| Sales | | 243,775 |
| Cost of sales | | 152,425 |
| Gross profit | | X |
| Other income | | 3,500 |
| | | X |
| Selling and distribution expenses | 25,725 | |
| Administration expenses | 25,900 | |
| Finance expenses | 29,225 | |
| | | X |
| Net profit | | X |

***Task***

Fill in the missing numbers in the spaces marked with an 'X'. Start with the balance sheet and work down as far as 'net assets'. Insert this figure in the space labelled 'capital as at 30 April 20X7'. You should then be able to work out the other missing numbers.

*Helping hand.* Before looking at the solution, check for yourself whether your answer is right by comparing the 'net profit' figure in the profit and loss account with the 'profit for the year' figure in the balance sheet. If your answer is correct, the two figures should be the same.

## 4 DOCUMENTING BUSINESS TRANSACTIONS

4.1 Whenever a business transaction is carried out, one or more of the following documents might be used. You should be able to describe their purpose, function and usual contents.

- Invoice
- Credit note
- Letter of enquiry
- Quotation
- Sales/purchase order
- Stock lists
- Supplier lists
- Staff time sheets
- Goods received/delivered notes
- Till receipts

> These two are the most important. Learn their contents in detail. They may be used in multi-part stationery sets.

---

**Activity 1.4**

List the documents which you would expect to change hands when you have a new roof installed in your house.

---

4.2 The purpose of the **accounting system** is to record, summarise and present the information contained in the documentation generated by transactions.

## Discounts

4.3 There are two types of discount which you must be able to deal with.

- **Trade discounts** (a reduction in the cost of the goods)
- **Cash discounts** (a reduction in the amount payable for the goods)

---

**Activity 1.5**

You are employed by a company which distributes electrical goods to electrical shops and other retail outlets. You receive a telephone call from John Smith, the proprietor of Smith Electrical, who is interested in purchasing 60 of the new halogen toasters which you are stocking. The toasters normally sell for £50 but you are able to offer a 20% trade discount and in addition a settlement discount of 5%, provided that payment is made within 14 days. John Smith asks you to give him a verbal quotation of exactly how much he would have to pay for the toasters.

**Tasks**

(a) Clearly showing your workings, calculate how much in total Smith Electrical would have to pay for the toasters if payment was made within 14 days of the sale. Ignore VAT.

(b) Calculate how much would have to be paid if payment was *not* made within 14 days. Ignore VAT.

---

## VAT

4.4 Students often have problems with value added tax (VAT), but the rules for the types of transactions you will deal with are very straightforward.

| | |
|---|---|
| ***Rule 1*** | **There are two rates of VAT: standard rate (nearly always 17½%) and zero rate.** |
| ***Rule 2*** | Input tax **is paid on goods and services bought by a business;** output tax **is charged on goods and services sold.** |

| | |
|---|---|
| *Rule 3* | **Some goods are exempt from VAT.** |
| *Rule 4* | **Gross price = net price + VAT.** |
| *Rule 5* | **VAT included in a gross price can be calculated using the VAT fraction: 17.5/117.5 or 7/47.** |
| *Rule 6* | **Total VAT shown on an invoice should be rounded down to the nearest 1p, so £32.439 would be shown as £32.43.** |

**CENTRAL ASSESSMENT ALERT**

VAT, other than the double entry aspects, will not be tested in a Central Assessment, but you will need to know it for your portfolio,

*VAT and discounts*

4.5 When a cash discount is offered, VAT is computed on the amount of the invoice *less* the discount (at the highest rate offered), even if the discount is not taken.

### Activity 1.6

Electromarket Ltd, an electrical goods retailer, ordered 20 clock radios from Timewatch Ltd. The radios cost £10 each, plus VAT at 17.5%. By mistake, Timewatch Ltd supplied 25 clock radios and issued an invoice for 25. On being informed of its mistake, Timewatch issued a credit note for the 5 radios which were returned.

*Tasks*

(a) Design an invoice to reflect the original supply, adding further details which you think should appear.

(b) Design a credit note to reflect the goods returned.

*Helping hand.* Some of the details will be the same.

## Key learning points

- 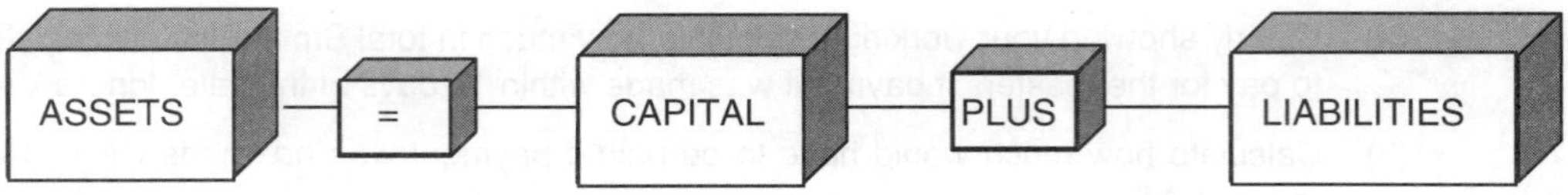


- Every transaction gives rise to:

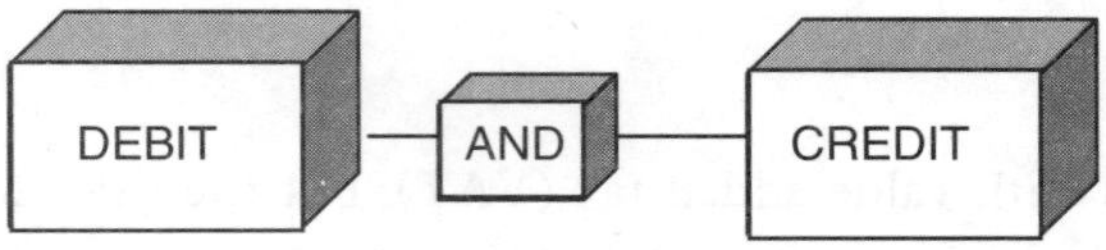


- P = I + D – C
  If you don't know what these mean, look back to paragraph 2.4.
- A **balance sheet** shows the assets, liabilities and capital at a given moment in time.
- The **profit and loss account** matches revenue earned with costs incurred in earning it.

- **Capital expenditure** is expenditure to improve or acquire fixed assets. It creates or increases fixed assets in the balance sheet.
- **Revenue expenditure** is for maintenance or the trade of the business. It is charged to the profit and loss account.

## Quick quiz

1 What is the accounting equation?

2 What is the business equation?

3 What is a balance sheet?

4 Name two types of discount and distinguish between them.

## Answers to quick quiz

1 Assets = Capital + Liabilities

2 Profit = Increase in net assets plus drawings less capital introduced

3 A balance sheet is a statement of the assets, liabilities and capital of a business at a given moment in time.

4 (i) Trade discount is a reduction in the cost of goods.
(ii) Cash discount is a reduction in the amount payable for the goods.

# 2 Recording, summarising and posting transactions

## This chapter contains



## Learning objectives

On completion of this chapter you will be able to:

- Post transactions from primary records to ledger accounts
- Understand the main types of ledger account

## Performance criteria

3.1 Details from the relevant primary documentation are recorded in the cash book

3.1 Totals and balances of receipts and payments are correctly calculated

3.2 Relevant accounts are totalled

## Range statement

3.2.1 Ledgers: main ledger, sub ledger, integrated ledger

## Knowledge and understanding

- Relationship between the accounting system and the ledger
- Methods of posting from primary records to ledger accounts
- Inter-relationship of accounts – double entry system

# 1 INTRODUCTION

1.1 This is an important chapter – if you can get the hang of ledger accounting and double entry, you'll be on course for your later studies. Don't worry if it seems tricky at first – lots of people take a while to get used to it. Just go slowly and carefully.

# 2 RECORDING BUSINESS TRANSACTIONS: AN OVERVIEW

## Source documents

### KEY TERM

**Source documents** are the source of all the information recorded by a business.

2.1 You have already come across source documents in your studies for Units 1 and 2. Just to recap, they are:

- Invoices
- Credit notes
- Petty cash vouchers
- Cheques received
- Cheque stubs (for cheques paid out)
- Wages, salaries and PAYE records

## Why do we need to record source documents?

2.2 During the course of its business, a company sends out and receives *many* source documents. The details on these source documents need to be recorded, otherwise the business might forget to ask for some money, or forget to pay some, or even accidentally pay something twice. In other words, it needs to **keep records of source documents** - of transactions - so that it can keep tabs on what is going on.

## How do we record them?

2.3 In **books of prime entry**.

### KEY TERM

**Books of prime entry** form the record of all the documented transactions sent and received by the company. They are as follows.

| Book of prime entry | Documents recorded | Summarised and posted to |
|---|---|---|
| Sales day book | Sales invoices, credit notes sent | Sales ledger/control account |
| Purchase day book | Purchase invoices, credit notes received | Purchases ledger/control account |
| Cash book | Cash paid and received | Main ledger |
| Petty cash book | Notes and coin paid and received | Main ledger |
| Journal | Adjustments | Main ledger |

### Activity 2.1

State which books of prime entry the following transactions would be entered into.

(a) Your business pays A Brown (a supplier) £450.
(b) You send D Steptoe (a customer) an invoice for £650.
(c) You receive an invoice from A Brown for £300.
(d) You pay D Steptoe £500.
(e) F Jones (a customer) returns goods to the value of £250.
(f) You return goods to J Green to the value of £504.
(g) F Jones pays you £500.

### TERMINOLOGY ALERT

The AAT uses specific terminology.

**Main ledger** - this is the same as **general or nominal ledger**.

**Subsidiary ledger** - this is the same as:

- **Sales (debtors ledger) AND**
- **Purchases (creditors ledger)**

In this text we will use sales (debtors) and purchases (creditors) ledger rather than subsidiary ledger because you need to tell them apart. But be prepared to meet 'subsidiary ledger' in a central assessment.

## Summarising source documents

2.4 Because of the volume of source documents, and the fact that they come from and are sent to a very large number of suppliers and customers, it is vital that the information in them is **summarised.** This is done in two ways.

| Ledger used | Need for summary |
|---|---|
| *Subsidiary ledgers*<br>Sales ledger<br>Purchase ledger | Summaries need to be kept of all the transactions undertaken with an **individual** supplier or customer - invoices, credit notes, cash - so that a net amount due or owed can be calculated. |
| *Main ledger*<br>(a) Sales ledger control account<br>(b) Purchase ledger control account | Summaries need to be kept of **all** the transactions undertaken with all suppliers and customers, so a total for debtors and a total for creditors can be calculated. |

We will look at control accounts in more detail later in this Text.

## Posting the ledgers

2.5 Have a look at the diagram on the next page. It shows how items are **posted** to (**entered in**) the ledgers, ultimately to arrive at the financial statements. Don't worry that some of the terms are unfamiliar currently - you will be able to trace through what is going on when you have completed this Text.

**CENTRAL ASSESSMENT ALERT**

A great deal of the material covered in this chapter appears in various forms throughout the Central Assessment. You must understand all the principles laid out in this chapter.

# 3 THE SALES DAY BOOK

**KEY TERM**

The **sales day book** is a list of all invoices sent out to **customers** each day.

3.1 An extract from a sales day book, ignoring VAT for the moment, might look like this.

SALES DAY BOOK

| *Date* | *Invoice number (2)* | *Customer* | *Sales ledger folio (1)* | *Total amount invoiced* |
|---|---|---|---|---|
| 20X7 | | | | £ |
| Jan 10 | 247 | James Ltd | SL14 | 105.00 |
| | 248 | Steptoe & Son | SL 8 | 86.40 |
| | 249 | Talbot & Co | SL 6 | 31.80 |
| | 250 | John Silvertown | SL 9 | 1,264.60 |
| | | | | 1,487.80 |

(1) The column called 'sales ledger folio' is a reference to a page (by convention called a folio) for the individual customer in the **sales ledger**. It means, for example, that the sale to James Ltd for £105 is also recorded on page 14 of the sales ledger.

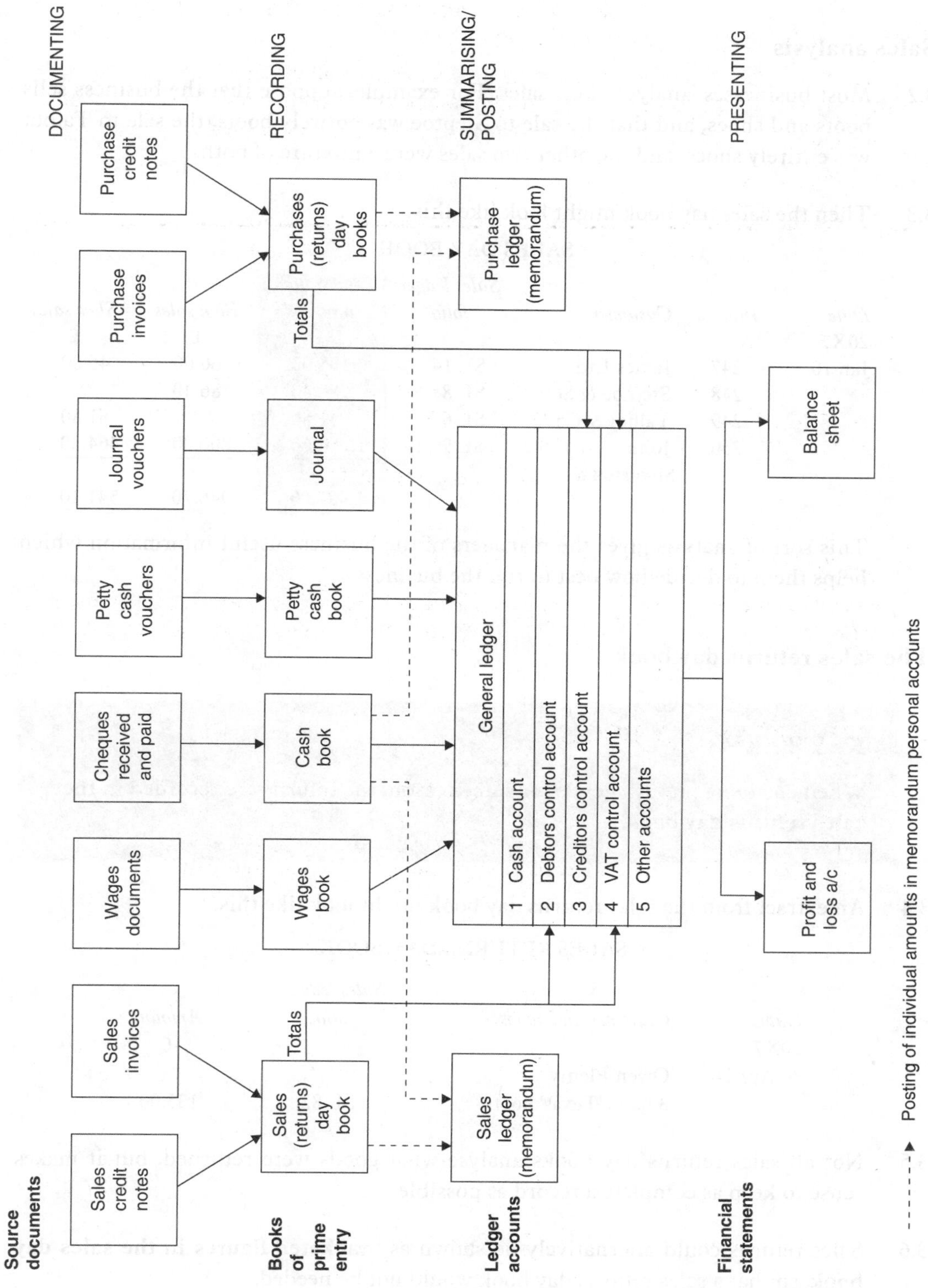
DOCUMENTING
RECORDING
SUMMARISING/POSTING
PRESENTING
Source documents
Sales credit notes
Sales invoices
Wages documents
Cheques received and paid
Petty cash vouchers
Journal vouchers
Purchase invoices
Purchase credit notes
Books of prime entry
Sales (returns) day book
Totals
Wages book
Cash book
Petty cash book
Journal
Purchases (returns) day books
Totals
Ledger accounts
Sales ledger (memorandum)
General ledger
1 Cash account
2 Debtors control account
3 Creditors control account
4 VAT control account
5 Other accounts
Purchase ledger (memorandum)
Financial statements
Profit and loss a/c
Balance sheet
Posting of individual amounts in memorandum personal accounts

(2) The invoice number is the **unique number** given to each sales invoice by the business's sales system. Listing them out sequentially in the sales day book helps us to see that all the invoices are included.

## Sales analysis

3.2 Most businesses 'analyse' their sales. For example, suppose that the business sells boots and shoes, and that the sale to Steptoe was entirely boots, the sale to Talbot was entirely shoes, and the other two sales were a mixture of both.

3.3 Then the sales day book might look like this.

SALES DAY BOOK

| *Date* | *Invoice* | *Customer* | *Sales ledger folio* | *Total amount invoiced* | *Boot sales* | *Shoe sales* |
|---|---|---|---|---|---|---|
| 20X7 | | | | £ | £ | £ |
| Jan 10 | 247 | James Ltd | SL 14 | 105.00 | 60.00 | 45.00 |
| | 248 | Steptoe & Son | SL 8 | 86.40 | 86.40 | |
| | 249 | Talbot & Co | SL 6 | 31.80 | | 31.80 |
| | 250 | John Silvertown | SL 9 | 1,264.60 | 800.30 | 464.30 |
| | | | | 1,487.80 | 946.70 | 541.10 |

This sort of analysis gives the managers of the business useful information which helps them to decide how best to run the business.

## The sales returns day book

**KEY TERM**

When customers return goods for some reason, the returns are recorded in the **sales returns day book**.

3.4 An extract from the sales returns day book might look like this.

SALES RETURNS DAY BOOK

| *Date* | *Customer and goods* | *Sales ledger folio* | *Amount* |
|---|---|---|---|
| 20X7 | | | £ |
| 30 April | Owen Plenty<br>3 pairs 'Texas' boots | SL 82 | 135.00 |

3.5 Not all sales returns day books analyse what goods were returned, but it makes sense to keep as complete a record as possible.

3.6 Sales returns could alternatively be shown as **bracketed figures in the sales day book**, so that a sales returns day book would not be needed.

## 4 THE PURCHASE DAY BOOK

**KEY TERM**

The **purchase day book** is the record of all the invoices received from **suppliers.**

4.1 An extract from a purchase day book might look like this (again, we have ignored VAT).

PURCHASE DAY BOOK

| *Date* | *Supplier (2)* | *Purchase ledger folio (1)* | *Total amount invoiced* | *Purchases (3)* | *Expenses* |
|---|---|---|---|---|---|
| 20X7 | | | £ | £ | £ |
| Mar 15 | Sugar & Spice | PL 31 | 315.00 | 315.00 | |
| | F Seager | PL 46 | 29.40 | 29.40 | |
| | ABC | PL 42 | 116.80 | | 116.80 |
| | Shabnum Rashid | PL 12 | 100.00 | 100.00 | |
| | | | 561.20 | 444.40 | 116.80 |

(1) The 'purchase ledger folio' is a reference to a page for the individual supplier in the purchase ledger.

(2) There is no 'invoice number' column, because the purchase day book records **other people's invoices**, which have all sorts of different numbers. Sometimes, however, a purchase day book may allocate an internal number to an invoice.

(3) Like the sales day book, the purchase day book analyses the invoices which have been sent in. In this example, three of the invoices related to goods which the business intends to re-sell (called simply 'purchases') and the fourth invoice was an electricity bill.

### The purchase returns day book

**KEY TERM**

The **purchase returns day book** is kept to record credit notes received in respect of goods which the business sends back to its suppliers.

4.2 The business might expect a **credit note** from the supplier. In the meantime, however, it might issue a debit note to the supplier, indicating the amount by which the business expects its total debt to the supplier to be reduced.

An extract from the purchase returns day book might look like this.

PURCHASE RETURNS DAY BOOK

| *Date* | *Supplier and goods* | *Purchase ledger folio* | *Amount* |
|---|---|---|---|
| 20X7 | | | £ |
| 29 April | Boxes Ltd | | |
| | 300 cardboard boxes | PL 123 | 46.60 |

4.3 Again, purchase returns could be shown as **bracketed figures** in the purchase day book.

## 5 THE CASH BOOK

5.1 You have already come across the cash book in your Unit 1 studies. Here we are concerned with the accounting aspects.

**KEY TERM**

The **cash book** is a book of prime entry, used to keep a cumulative record of money received and money paid out by the business via its bank account.

5.2 This could be money received **on the business premises** in notes, coins and cheques which are subsequently banked. There are also receipts and payments made by bank transfer, standing order, direct debit, BACS and, in the case of bank interest and charges, directly by the bank.

5.3 One part of the cash book is used to record **receipts of cash**, and another part is used to **record payments**. Below is a summary of what a cash book looks like

| LEFT HAND SIDE: RECEIPTS | | | | | RIGHT HAND SIDE: PAYMENTS | | | | |
|---|---|---|---|---|---|---|---|---|---|
| *Date* | *Narrative* | *Discount allowed* | *Receipt* | *Analysis* | *Date* | *Narrative* | *Discount received* | *Payment* | *Analysis* |
| | | £10 | £100 | £100 | | | £7 | £90 | £90 |

Note the following points about this cash book.

(a) It represents two sides of a **ledger account**: the left hand receipts side is DEBIT, the right hand payments side is CREDIT (see Section 6 below).

(b) It is a **two-column cash book -** on the debit side there are two columns: one column for total receipts and one for discounts allowed; on the credit side there are also two columns – one for total payments and one for discounts received.

(c) Discounts allowed (given) and received are **memorandum columns** only - they do not represent cash movements.

(d) On each side, the 'analysis' can be one or more columns; **the total of the analysis columns *always* equals the total receipts or total payments.**

5.4 The best way to see how the cash book works is to follow through an example. **Note that in this example we are continuing to ignore VAT.**

### 5.5 EXAMPLE: CASH BOOK

At the beginning of 1 September, Liz Cullis had £900 in the bank. During 1 September 20X7, Liz Cullis had the following receipts and payments.

(a) Cash sale: receipt of £80
(b) Payment from credit customer Hay: £400 less discount allowed £20
(c) Payment from credit customer Been: £720

(d) Payment from credit customer Seed: £1,000 less discount allowed £40
(e) Cash sale: receipt of £150
(f) Cash received for sale of machine: £200
(g) Payment to supplier Kew: £120
(h) Payment to supplier Hare: £310
(i) Payment of telephone bill: £400
(j) Payment of gas bill: £280
(k) Payment of £1,500 to Hess for new plant and machinery

If you look through these transactions, you will see that six of them are receipts and five of them are payments.

## 5.6 SOLUTION

The cash book for Liz Cullis would be as shown on the following page.

5.7 In a standard two-column cash book:

- Receipts and payments are listed out on either side of the cash book - **receipts** on the **left** (debit **asset**) and **payments** on the **right** (credit **asset**).
- Both sides have columns for these details.
  - Date
  - Narrative
  - Folio reference
  - **Total**
  - **Discount allowed/received**
- Each side has a number of **columns for further analysis** - receipts from debtors, cash sales and other receipts; payments to creditors, expenses and fixed assets for payments.

## Balancing the cash book

5.8 At the beginning of the day there is a debit **opening balance** of £900 on Liz Cullis' cash book. During the day, the total receipts and payments were as follows.

| | £ |
|---|---|
| Opening balance | 900 |
| Receipts | 2,490 |
| | 3,390 |
| Payments | (2,610) |
| Closing balance | 780 |

The **closing balance** of £780 represents the excess of receipts over payments. It means that Liz Cullis still has cash available at the end of the day, so he 'carries it down' at the end of 1 September from the payments side of the cash book, and 'brings it down' at the beginning of 2 September to the receipts side of the cash book.

## LIZ CULLIS: CASH BOOK

RECEIPTS

| Date | Narrative | Folio | Discount allowed | Total | Receipts from debtors | Cash sales | Other |
|---|---|---|---|---|---|---|---|
| 20X7 | | | £ | £ | £ | £ | £ |
| 01-Sep | Balance b/d (= opening bal) | | | 900 | | | |
| | (a) Cash sale | | | 80 | | 80 | |
| | (b) Debtor pays: Hay | SL96 | 20 | 380 | 380 | | |
| | (c) Debtor pays: Been | SL632 | | 720 | 720 | | |
| | (d) Debtor pays: Seed | SL501 | 40 | 960 | 960 | | |
| | (e) Cash sale | | | 150 | | 150 | |
| | (f) Fixed asset sale | | | 200 | | | 200 |
| | | | 60 | 3,390 | 2,060 | 230 | 200 |
| 02-Sep | Balance b/d (= new opening bal) | | | 780 | | | |

PAYMENTS

| Date | Narrative | Folio | Total | Payments to creditors | Expenses | Fixed assets |
|---|---|---|---|---|---|---|
| 20X7 | | | | | | |
| 01-Sep | (g) Creditor paid: Kew | PL543 | 120 | 120 | | |
| | (h) Creditor paid: Hare | PL76 | 310 | 310 | | |
| | (i) Telephone expense | | 400 | | 400 | |
| | (j) Gas expense | | 280 | | 280 | |
| | (k) Plant & machinery | | 1,500 | | | 1,500 |
| | | | 2,610 | 430 | 680 | 1,500 |
| | Balance c/d (= closing bal) | | 780 | | | |
| | | | 3,390 | 430 | 680 | 1,500 |

**TERMINOLOGY ALERT**

Accountants generally use the terminology 'balance brought down' or 'balance b/d' and 'balance carried down' or 'balance c/d' instead of 'opening balance' and 'closing balance'.

| | | |
|---|---|---|
| Balance b/d | Balance brought down | Opening balance |
| Balance c/d | Balance carried down | Closing balance |

## Bank statements

5.9 Weekly or monthly, a business will receive a **bank statement**. Bank statements should be used to check that the amount shown as a balance in the cash book agrees with the amount on the bank statement, and that no cash has 'gone missing'.

## Petty cash book

5.10 This is for small items. You have already covered it.

**KEY TERM**

The **petty cash book** is the book of prime entry which keeps a cumulative record of the small amounts of cash received into and paid out of the cash float.

# 6 THE MAIN LEDGER

**KEY TERM**

The **main ledger** is the accounting record which summarises the financial affairs of a business. It contains details of assets, liabilities and capital, income and expenditure and so profit and loss. It consists of a large number of different **ledger accounts**, each account having its own purpose or 'name' and an identity or code. Other names for the main ledger are the **nominal ledger** or **general ledger**.

6.1 Transactions are **posted** to accounts in the main ledger from the books of prime entry.

**KEY TERM**

**Posting** means to enter transactions in ledger accounts in the main ledger from books of prime entry. Often this is done in total (ie all sales invoices in the sales day book for a day are added up and the total is posted to the debtors control account) but individual transactions are also posted (eg fixed assets).

6.2 Here are some examples of ledger accounts in the main ledger.

| Ledger account | Fixed asset | Current asset | Current liability | Long-term liability | Capi-tal | Expense | Income |
|---|---|---|---|---|---|---|---|
| Plant and machinery at cost | √ | | | | | | |
| Motor vehicles at cost | √ | | | | | | |
| Proprietor's capital | | | | | √ | | |
| Purchases: raw materials | | √ | | | | | |
| Purchases: finished goods | | √ | | | | | |
| Debtors control | | √ | | | | | |
| Creditors control | | | √ | | | | |
| Wages and salaries | | | | | | √ | |
| Rent and rates | | | | | | √ | |
| Advertising expenses | | | | | | √ | |
| Bank charges | | | | | | √ | |
| Motor expenses | | | | | | √ | |
| Telephone expenses | | | | | | √ | |
| Sales | | | | | | | √ |
| Cash | | √ | | | | | |
| Bank overdraft | | | √ | | | | |
| Bank loan | | | | √ | | | |

## The format of a ledger account

6.3 If a ledger account were to be kept in an actual book rather than as a computer record, its **format** might be as follows.

ADVERTISING EXPENSES

| *Date* | *Narrative* | *Folio* | £ | *Date* | *Narrative* | *Folio* | £ |
|---|---|---|---|---|---|---|---|
| 20X7 | | | | | | | |
| 15 April | AbFab Agency for quarter to 31 March | PL 348 | 2,500 | | | | |

There are two sides to the account, and an account heading on top, and so it is convenient to think in terms of 'T' accounts:

- On top of the account is its name
- There is a left hand side, or **debit** side
- There is a right hand side, or **credit** side

NAME OF ACCOUNT

| DEBIT SIDE | £ | CREDIT SIDE | £ |
|---|---|---|---|
| | | | |

6.4 We have already seen this with Liz Cullis's cash book. We will now go on to use the cash book to demonstrate double-entry.

# 7 DOUBLE ENTRY BOOK-KEEPING

7.1 **Every financial transaction gives rise to two accounting entries, one a debit and the other a credit.**

| **DEBIT**<br>To own/have<br>↓ | **CREDIT**<br>To owe<br>↓ |
|---|---|
| AN ASSET INCREASES<br>eg new office furniture | AN ASSET DECREASES<br>eg pay out cash |
| CAPITAL/ A LIABILITY DECREASES<br>eg pay a creditor | CAPITAL/A LIABILITY INCREASES<br>eg buy goods on credit |
| INCOME DECREASES<br>eg cancel a sale | INCOME INCREASES<br>eg make a sale |
| AN EXPENSE INCREASES<br>eg incur advertising costs | AN EXPENSE DECREASES<br>eg cancel a purchase |
| **Left hand side** | **Right hand side** |

## Cash transactions: double entry

7.2 The cash book is a good starting point for understanding double entry. Remember:

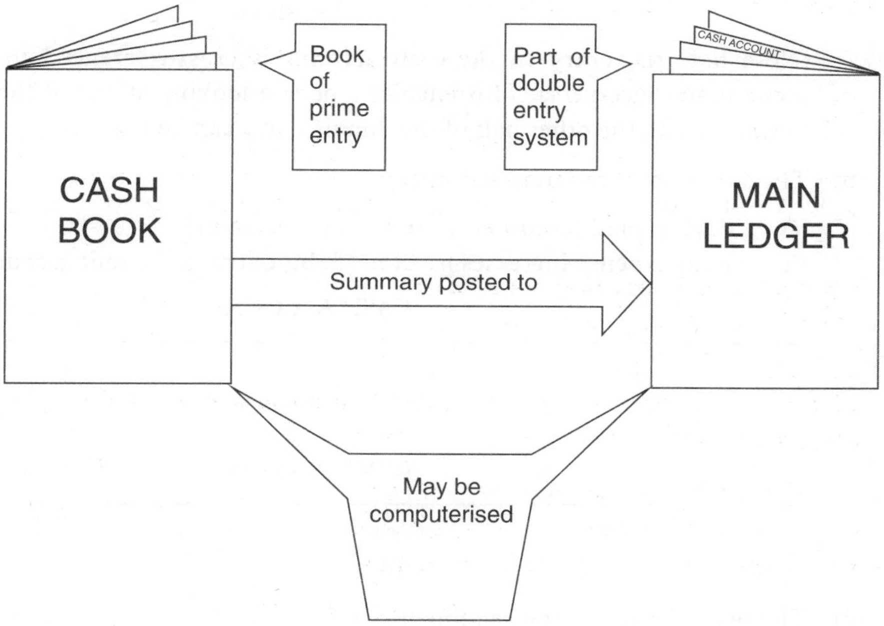


7.3 Here are the main cash transactions.

| Cash transactions | DR | CR |
|---|---|---|
| Sell goods for cash | Cash | Sales |
| Buy goods for cash | Purchases | Cash |
| Pay an expense | Expense a/c | Cash |

## 7.4 EXAMPLE: DOUBLE ENTRY FOR CASH TRANSACTIONS

In the cash book of a business, the following transactions have been recorded.

(a) A cash sale (ie a receipt) of £2
(b) Payment of a rent bill totalling £150
(c) Buying some goods for cash at £100
(d) Buying some shelves for cash at £200

How would these four transactions be posted to the ledger accounts? For that matter, which ledger accounts should they be posted to? Don't forget that each transaction will be posted twice, in accordance with the rule of double entry.

## 7.5 SOLUTION

(a) The two sides of the transaction are:

(i) Cash is received (**debit** entry in the cash account)
(ii) Sales increase by £2 (**credit** entry in the sales account)

CASH ACCOUNT

| | £ | | £ |
|---|---|---|---|
| Sales a/c | 2 | | |

SALES ACCOUNT

| | £ | | £ |
|---|---|---|---|
| | | Cash a/c | 2 |

(Note how the entry in the cash account is cross-referenced to the sales account and vice-versa. This enables a person looking at one of the accounts to trace where the other half of the double entry can be found.)

(b) The two sides of the transaction are:

(i) Cash is paid (**credit** entry in the cash account)
(ii) Rent expense increases by £150 (**debit** entry in the rent account)

CASH ACCOUNT

| | £ | | £ |
|---|---|---|---|
| | | Rent a/c | 150 |

RENT ACCOUNT

| | £ | | £ |
|---|---|---|---|
| Cash a/c | 150 | | |

(c) The two sides of the transaction are:

(i) Cash is paid (**credit** entry in the cash account)
(ii) Purchases increase by £100 (**debit** entry in the purchases account)

CASH ACCOUNT

| | £ | | £ |
|---|---|---|---|
| | | Purchases a/c | 100 |

PURCHASES ACCOUNT

| | | | |
|---|---|---|---|
| | £ | | 77 |
| Cash a/c | 100 | | |

(d) The two sides of the transaction are:

(i) Cash is paid (**credit** entry in the cash account)

(ii) Assets - in this case, shelves - increase by £200 (**debit** entry in shelves account)

CASH ACCOUNT

| | | | |
|---|---|---|---|
| | £ | | £ |
| | | Shelves a/c | 200 |

SHELVES (ASSET) ACCOUNT

| | | | |
|---|---|---|---|
| | £ | | £ |
| Cash a/c | 200 | | |

If all four of these transactions related to the same business, the **summary cash account** of that business would end up looking like this.

CASH ACCOUNT

| | | | |
|---|---|---|---|
| | £ | | £ |
| Sales a/c | 2 | Rent a/c | 150 |
| | | Purchases a/c | 100 |
| | | Shelves a/c | 200 |

### Activity 2.2

In the cash book of a business, the following transactions have been recorded on 7 April 20X7.

(a) A cash sale (ie a receipt) of £60
(b) Payment of rent totalling £4,500 (no invoice was received)
(c) Buying some goods for cash at £3,000
(d) Buying some shelves for cash at £6,000

**Task**

Draw the appropriate ledger ('T') accounts and show how these four transactions would be posted to them.

## Credit transactions: double entry

7.6 Not all transactions are settled immediately in cash.

(a) A business might purchase goods from its suppliers on **credit terms**, so that the suppliers would be **creditors** of the business until settlement was made in cash.

(b) The business might grant credit terms to its customers who would then be **debtors** of the business.

Clearly no entries can be made in the cash book when a credit transaction occurs, because initially no cash has been received or paid. Where then can the details of the transactions be entered?

7.7 The solution to this problem is to use **ledger accounts for debtors and creditors.**

| CREDIT TRANSACTIONS | DR | CR |
|---|---|---|
| Sell goods on credit terms | Debtors | Sales |
| Receive cash from debtor | Cash | Debtors |
| Net effect = cash transaction | Cash | Sales |
| Buy goods on credit terms | Purchases | Creditors |
| Pay cash to creditor | Creditors | Cash |
| Net effect = cash transaction | Purchases | Cash |

The net effect in the ledger accounts is the same as for a cash transaction - the only difference is that there has been a time delay during which the debtor/creditor accounts have been used.

## 7.8 EXAMPLE: CREDIT TRANSACTIONS

Recorded in the sales day book and the purchase day book are the following transactions.

(a) The business sells goods on credit to a customer Mr A for £2,000.
(b) The business buys goods on credit from a supplier B Ltd for £100.

How and where are these transactions posted in the ledger accounts?

## 7.9 SOLUTION

(a) DEBTORS ACCOUNT

| | £ | | £ |
|---|---|---|---|
| Sales a/c | 2,000 | | |

SALES ACCOUNT

| | £ | | £ |
|---|---|---|---|
| | | Debtors account (Mr A) | 2,000 |

(b) CREDITORS ACCOUNT

| | £ | | £ |
|---|---|---|---|
| | | Purchases a/c | 100 |

PURCHASES ACCOUNT

| | £ | | £ |
|---|---|---|---|
| Creditors a/c (B Ltd) | 100 | | |

## 7.10 EXAMPLE CONTINUED: WHEN CASH IS PAID TO CREDITORS OR BY DEBTORS

Suppose that, in the example above, the business paid £100 to B Ltd one month after the goods were acquired. The two sides of this new transaction are:

(a) Cash is paid (**credit** entry in the cash account).

(b) The amount owing to creditors is reduced (**debit** entry in the creditors account).

CASH ACCOUNT

| | | | |
|---|---|---|---|
| | £ | | £ |
| | | Creditors a/c (B Ltd) | 100 |

CREDITORS ACCOUNT

| | | | |
|---|---|---|---|
| | £ | | £ |
| Cash a/c | 100 | | |

7.11 If we now bring together the two parts of this example, the original purchase of goods on credit and the eventual settlement in cash, we find that the accounts appear as follows.

CASH ACCOUNT

| | | | |
|---|---|---|---|
| | £ | | £ |
| | | Creditors a/c | 100 |

PURCHASES ACCOUNT

| | | | |
|---|---|---|---|
| | £ | | £ |
| Creditors a/c | 100 | | |

CREDITORS ACCOUNT

| | | | |
|---|---|---|---|
| | £ | | £ |
| Cash a/c | 100 | Purchases a/c | 100 |

7.12 The **two entries in the creditors account cancel each other out,** indicating that no money is owing to creditors any more. We are left with a credit entry of £100 in the cash account and a debit entry of £100 in the purchases account. These are exactly the entries which would have been made to record a **cash** purchase of £100.

7.13 Similar reasoning applies when a **customer settles his debt.** In the example above when Mr A pays his debt of £2,000 the two sides of the transaction are:

- Cash is received (debit entry in the cash account)
- The amount owed by debtors is reduced (credit entry in the debtors account)

CASH ACCOUNT

| | | | |
|---|---|---|---|
| | £ | | £ |
| Debtors a/c (Mr A) | 2,000 | | |

DEBTORS ACCOUNT

| | | | |
|---|---|---|---|
| | £ | | £ |
| | | Cash a/c | 2,000 |

The accounts recording this sale to, and payment by, Mr A now appear as follows.

CASH ACCOUNT

| | | | |
|---|---|---|---|
| | £ | | £ |
| Debtors a/c | 2,000 | | |

SALES ACCOUNT

| | | | |
|---|---|---|---|
| | £ | | £ |
| | | Debtors a/c | 2,000 |

DEBTORS ACCOUNT

| | | | |
|---|---|---|---|
| | £ | | £ |
| Sales a/c | 2,000 | Cash a/c | 2,000 |

7.14 The **two entries in the debtors account cancel each other out,** while the entries in the cash account and sales account reflect the same position as if the sale had been made for cash.

### Activity 2.3

Identify the debit and credit entries in the following transactions.

(a) Bought a machine on credit from A, cost £8,000
(b) Bought goods on credit from B, cost £500
(c) Sold goods on credit to C, value £1,200
(d) Paid D (a creditor) £300
(e) Collected £180 from E, a debtor
(f) Paid wages £4,000
(g) Received rent bill of £700 from landlord G
(h) Paid rent of £700 to landlord G
(i) Paid insurance premium £90

### Activity 2.4

Your business, which is not registered for VAT, has the following transactions.

(a) The sale of goods on credit
(b) Credit notes to credit customers upon the return of faulty goods
(c) Daily cash takings paid into the bank

**Task**

For each transaction identify clearly:

(a) The original document(s)
(b) The book of prime entry for the transaction
(c) The way in which the data will be incorporated into the double entry system

## 8 POSTING FROM THE DAY BOOKS

### Sales day book to debtors control account

8.1 Earlier we used four transactions entered into the sales day book.

SALES DAY BOOK

| *Date* | *Invoice* | *Customer* | *Sales ledger folios* | *Total amount invoiced* | *Boot sales* | *Shoe sales* |
|---|---|---|---|---|---|---|
| 20X7 | | | | £ | £ | £ |
| Jan 10 | 247 | James Ltd | SL 14 | 105.00 | 60.00 | 45.00 |
| | 248 | Steptoe & Son | SL 8 | 86.40 | 86.40 | |
| | 249 | Talbot & Co | SL 6 | 31.80 | | 31.80 |
| | 250 | John Silvertown | SL 9 | 1,264.60 | 800.30 | 464.30 |
| | | | | 1,487.80 | 946.70 | 541.10 |

8.2 How do we post these transactions to the main ledger, and which accounts do we use in the main ledger?

8.3 We would post the total of the **total amount invoiced column** to the **debit** side of the **debtors control account** (often called the **sales ledger control account**). The **credit** entries would be to the different **sales accounts,** in this case, boot sales and shoe sales.

DEBTORS CONTROL ACCOUNT

| | £ | | £ |
|---|---|---|---|
| Boot sales | 946.70 | | |
| Shoes sales | 541.10 | | |
| | 1,487.80 | | |

BOOT SALES

| | £ | | £ |
|---|---|---|---|
| | | Debtors control | 946.70 |

SHOE SALES

| | £ | | £ |
|---|---|---|---|
| | | Debtors control | 541.10 |

8.4 That is why the analysis of sales is kept, and why we analyse items in others books of prime entry.

8.5 So how do we know how much we are owed by individual debtors? The answer is that we keep two sets of accounts running in parallel - the **debtors control account** in the main ledger and the memorandum **sales ledger** (individual debtor accounts).

**REMEMBER!**

**Only the debtors control account is actually part of the double-entry system,** but **individual** debtors' transactions are posted to the sales ledger from the sales day book.

## Purchases day book to creditors control account

8.6 Here is the page of the purchases day book which we saw in Paragraph 4.1.

PURCHASE DAY BOOK

| *Date* | *Supplier* | *Purchase ledger folio)* | *Total amount invoiced* | *Purchases* | *Expenses* |
|---|---|---|---|---|---|
| 20X7 | | | £ | £ | £ |
| Mar 15 | Sugar & Spice | PL 31 | 315.00 | 315.00 | |
| | F Seager | PL 46 | 29.40 | 29.40 | |
| | ABC | PL 42 | 116.80 | | 116.80 |
| | Shabnum Rashid | PL 12 | 100.00 | 100.00 | |
| | | | 561.20 | 444.40 | 116.80 |

8.7 This time we will post the total of the total amount invoiced column to the credit side of the creditors control account (or purchase ledger control account) in the main ledger. The debit entries are to the different expense account, in this case purchases and electricity.

CREDITORS CONTROL ACCOUNT

| | £ | | £ |
|---|---|---|---|
| | | Purchases | 444.40 |
| | | Electricity | 116.80 |
| | | | 561.20 |

PURCHASES

| | £ | | £ |
|---|---|---|---|
| Creditors control | 444.40 | | |

ELECTRICITY

| | £ | | £ |
|---|---|---|---|
| Creditors control | 116.80 | | |

8.8 Again, we keep a separate record of how much we owe individual creditors by keeping two sets of accounts running in parallel - **the creditors control account** in the main ledger, part of the double-entry system, and the memorandum **purchase ledger** (individual creditors' accounts). We enter individual creditors' transactions in their purchase ledger account from the purchase day book.

### 8.9 Section summary

| **CREDIT TRANSACTIONS** | **DR** | | **CR** | |
|---|---|---|---|---|
| | *Memorandum* | *Main ledger** | *Main ledger** | *Memorandum* |
| Sell goods to John Silvertown | Sales ledger: John Silvertown | Debtors control a/c | Sales | - |
| Receive cash from John Silvertown | - | Cash a/c | Debtors control a/c | Sales ledger: John Silvertown |
| Buy goods from Sugar & Spice | - | Purchases | Creditors control a/c | Purchase ledger: Sugar & Spice |
| Pay cash to Sugar & Spice | Purchase ledger: Sugar & Spice | Creditors control a/c | Cash a/c | - |

*Individual transactions included in **totals** posted from books of prime entry.

8.10 Now you do some work! Have a go at these activities.

## Activity 2.5

Jane Smith is a sole trader. The various accounts used in her business are held in a cash book, a sales ledger, a purchase ledger and a nominal (general) ledger.

The following transactions take place.

(a) A cheque is issued to P Jones for £264 in payment for goods previously purchased on credit.

(b) An invoice for £850 is received from Davis Wholesalers Ltd relating to the supply of goods on credit.

(c) A credit note for £42 is received from K Williams in respect of goods returned.

(d) New fixtures costing £5,720 are purchased from Fixit Stores and paid for by cheque.

(e) An invoice for £25 relating to the delivery of the fixtures is received from Fixit Stores and settled immediately by cheque.

(f) G Cullis sells £85 of goods to Jane Smith for cash.

(g) An invoice is issued to R Newman for £340 relating to the purchase by him of goods on credit.

(h) An insurance premium of £64 is paid to Insureburn Ltd by cheque.

(i) A cheque for £40 received previously from J Baxter, a credit customer, is now returned unpaid by the bank.

**Task**

For each transaction in Jane Smith's books identify clearly:

(a) The name of the account to be debited
(b) The ledger in which the account to be debited would be located
(c) The name of the account to be credited
(d) The ledger in which the account to be credited would be located

Present your answer in the form of a table as follows.

| | *Account to be debited* | *Ledger* | *Accounted to be credited* | *Ledger* |
|---|---|---|---|---|
| (a) | | | | |
| (b) | | | | |
| etc | | | | |

## Activity 2.6

Your business has the following transactions.

(a) The purchase of goods on credit
(b) Allowances to credit customers upon the return of faulty goods
(c) Refund from petty cash to an employee of an amount spent on entertaining a client

**Task**

For each transaction identify clearly:

(i) The original document(s)
(ii) The book of prime entry for the transaction
(iii) The way in which the data will be incorporated into the double entry system

## Key learning points

- Business transactions are initially recorded on **source documents**. Records of the details on these documents are made in books of prime entry.
- The main **books of prime entry** are as follows.
  - Sales day book
  - Purchase day book
  - Journal
  - Cash book
  - Petty cash book
- Most accounts are contained in the **main ledger** (or **general or nominal ledger**).
- The rules of double entry state that every financial transaction gives rise to **two accounting entries,** one a **debit,** the other a **credit**. It is vital that you understand this principle.
- A **debit** is one of:
  - An increase in an asset
  - An increase in an expense
  - A decrease in a liability
- A **credit** is one of:
  - An increase in a liability
  - An increase in income
  - A decrease in an asset

## Quick quiz

1 What are books of prime entry?

2 What is recorded in the sales day book?

3 Does a debit entry on an asset account increase or decrease the asset?

4 What is the double entry when goods are sold for cash?

5 What is the double entry when goods are purchased on credit?

## Answers to quick quiz

1 Books of prime entry record all the documented transactions undertaken by the business.

2 The sales day book records the list of invoices sent out to customers each day.

3 It increases the asset balance.

4 *Debit* Cash; *Credit* Sales.

5 *Debit* Purchases; *Credit* Creditors account.

# 3 From ledger accounts to initial trial balance

**This chapter contains**



**Learning objectives**

On completion of this chapter you will be able to:

- Account for VAT
- Use the journal to record transactions and correct errors
- Prepare a trial balance
- Understand computerised and manual accounting systems

## Performance criteria

3.1 Totals and balances of receipts and payments are correctly calculated

3.1 Discrepancies are identified and referred to the appropriate person

3.2 Relevant accounts are totalled

3.2 Authorised adjustments are correctly processed and documented

3.3 Information required for the initial trial balance is identified and obtained from the relevant sources

3.3 Relevant people are asked for advice when the necessary information is not available

3.3 The draft initial trial balance is prepared in line with the organisation's policies and procedures

3.3 Discrepancies are identified in the balancing process and referred to the appropriate person

## Range statement

3.2.3 Adjustments to correct errors

3.3.1 Sources: colleagues; computer system; files; manager; accountant; ledger

3.3.2 Discrepancies: incorrect double entries; missing entries; wrong calculations

## Knowledge and understanding

- Operation of manual and computerised accounting systems
- Identification of different types of errors
- Inter-relationship of accounts – double entry system
- Use of journals
- Methods of closing off ledger accounts
- Function and form of the trial balance

## 1 INTRODUCTION

1.1 This chapter takes you from the ledger accounts to the trial balance, which is the stage before the final accounts. When you have worked through it, you will really feel that you are getting somewhere.

1.2 The chapter also touches on one or two other topics – accounting for VAT, the journal and computerised accounting systems.

## 2 ACCOUNTING FOR VAT

2.1 VAT was introduced in Unit 1. We now outline how VAT is accounted for. (The principles will be similar for most types of sales tax, in most countries, although the rates may differ.)

### Sales revenue

2.2 VAT charged is not kept - it is paid back to Customs & Excise. It follows that the **record of sales revenue should not include VAT.**

## 2.3 EXAMPLE: ACCOUNTING FOR OUTPUT VAT

If a business sells goods for £600 + £105 VAT, ie for £705 gross price, the sales account should only record the £600 excluding VAT. The accounting entries for the sale would be as follows.

| | | | |
|---|---|---|---|
| DEBIT | Cash **or** debtors | £705 | |
| CREDIT | Sales | | £600 |
| CREDIT | VAT account (output VAT) | | £105 |

2.4 Input VAT paid on purchases is not shown as a cost of the business - if it is reclaimed from C&E. However, input VAT is included in purchases if it is **not recoverable**.

(a) If input VAT is **recoverable**, the cost of purchases should exclude the VAT. If a business purchases goods on credit for £400 + recoverable VAT £70, the transaction would be recorded as follows.

| | | | |
|---|---|---|---|
| DEBIT | Purchases | £400 | |
| DEBIT | VAT account (input VAT) | £70 | |
| CREDIT | Trade creditors | | £470 |

(b) If the input VAT is **not recoverable,** the cost of purchases must include the tax, because it is the business itself which must bear the cost of the tax.

| | | | |
|---|---|---|---|
| DEBIT | Purchases | £470 | |
| CREDIT | Trade creditors | | £470 |

### When is VAT accounted for?

2.5 VAT is accounted for **when it first arises** - when recording **credit purchases/sales in credit transactions,** and when recording **cash received or paid in cash transactions.**

*VAT in credit transactions*

2.6 For credit sales the total amount invoiced, including VAT, will be recorded in the **sales day book**. The analysis columns separate the VAT from sales income as follows.

| *Date* | *Total* | *Sales income* | *VAT* |
|---|---|---|---|
| | £ | £ | £ |
| Johnson & Co | 2,350 | 2,000 | 350 |

2.7 Supplier invoices are recorded in total, including VAT, in the **purchase day book**. The analysis columns separate the recoverable input VAT from the purchase cost as follows.

| *Date* | *Total* | *Purchase cost* | *VAT* |
|---|---|---|---|
| | £ | £ | £ |
| Mayhew (Merchants) | 564 | 480 | 84 |

2.8 When debtors pay, or creditors are paid, there is no need to show the VAT in an analysis column of the cash book, because the VAT was recorded **when the sale or purchase was made, not when the debt was settled**.

*VAT in cash transactions*

2.9 VAT charged on **cash sales** or VAT paid on **cash purchases will be analysed in a separate column of the cash book**. Output VAT, having arisen from the cash sale, must be credited to the VAT account. Similarly, input VAT paid on cash purchases, must be debited to the VAT account.

### The VAT account

2.10 The VAT paid to or recovered from the authorities each quarter is the **balance on the VAT account**. This is the control account to which these items are posted.

- The total input VAT in the purchases day book (**debit**)
- The total output VAT in the sales day book (**credit**)
- VAT on cash sales (**credit**)
- VAT on cash purchases (**debit**)

## 2.11 EXAMPLE - VAT ACCOUNT

John Seager is registered for VAT.

(a) He is invoiced for input VAT of £175 on his credit purchases.
(b) He charges £450 VAT on his credit sales.
(c) He makes cash purchases including VAT of £22.30.
(d) He makes cash sales including VAT of £61.07.

Write up the VAT account.

## 2.12 SOLUTION

VAT ACCOUNT

| | £ | | £ |
|---|---|---|---|
| Purchase day book (input VAT) | 175.00 | Sales day book (output VAT) | 450.00 |
| Cash (input VAT) | 22.30 | | |
| | | Cash (output VAT) | 61.07 |
| Balance c/d (owed to Customs & Excise) | 313.76 | | |
| | 511.06 | | 511.07 |

2.13 Payments to or refunds from Customs and Excise do not usually coincide with the end of the accounting period of a business. At the balance sheet date there will be a VAT account balance. If this balance is for an amount **payable to** Customs and Excise, the outstanding creditor for VAT will appear as a **current liability** in the balance sheet.

2.14 Occasionally, a business will be **owed money** by Customs and Excise. In this case, the VAT refund owed by Customs and Excise would be a **current asset** in the balance sheet.

### Activity 3.1

Balvinder Patel runs a shop selling books, which are zero rated for value added tax (VAT), and other goods, on which standard rate VAT is chargeable at 17½%. No special retail scheme is operated and sales are all made in cash to the general public.

On 7 June 20X7, sales transactions were made with gross values (ie including VAT where applicable) as follows.

| Customer number | Gross sales value | Sales type* |
|---|---|---|
| | £ | |
| 1 | 72.06 | 1 |
| 2 | 48.00 | 2 |
| 3 | 4.25 | 2 |
| 3 | 11.70 | 1 |
| 4 | – 19.20 (refund) | 2 |
| 5 | 92.50 | 2 |
| 6 | 100.00 | 2 |
| 7 | 58.80 | 2 |
| 7 | 42.97 | 1 |
| 8 | 7.99 | 2 |
| 9 | 52.88 | 2 |
| 9 | – 8.40 (refund) | 1 |
| 10 | 23.50 | 2 |
| | 487.05 | |

* 1 = books; 2 = other goods

**Tasks**

(a) Calculate the amount of VAT arising from the day's sales and refund transactions for which Balvinder must account to HM Customs & Excise.

(b) State the ledger accounting entries to be made to record the transactions.

*Helping hand.* If you are in a hurry, don't worry too much about the different products.

## CENTRAL ASSESSMENT ALERT

Unless you are told otherwise you should make the following postings for VAT transactions.

| CREDIT TRANSACTIONS | DR | | CR | |
|---|---|---|---|---|
| | *Memorandum* | *Main ledger* | *Main ledger* | *Memorandum* |
| Sell goods on credit | Sales ledger 117.50 | Debtors control 117.50 | Sales 100.00<br>VAT 17.50 | - |
| Receive cash in settlement | - | Cash 117.50 | Debtors Control 117.50 | Sales ledger 117.50 |
| Buy goods on credit | - | Purchases 100.00<br>VAT 17.50 | Creditors Control 117.50 | Purchase ledger 117.50 |
| Pay cash in settlement | Purchase ledger 117.50 | Creditors control 117.50 | Cash 117.50 | - |
| **CASH TRANSACTIONS** | | | | |
| Sell goods for cash | - | Cash 117.50 | Sales 100.00<br>VAT 17.50 | - |
| Buy goods for cash | - | Purchases 100.00<br>VAT 17.50 | Cash 117.50 | - |

## 3 THE JOURNAL

3.1 One of the **books of prime entry** is the **journal**.

**KEY TERM**

The **journal** is a record of unusual movements between accounts. It records any double entries made which do not arise from the other books of prime entry.

3.2 Whatever type of transaction is being recorded, the **format of a journal entry** is:

| Date | | Folio | | |
|---|---|---|---|---|
| | | | £ | £ |
| DEBIT | Account to be debited | | X | |
| CREDIT | Account to be credited | | | X |
| *Narrative to explain the transaction* | | | | |

(Remember: the ledger accounts are written up to include the transactions listed in the journal.)

3.3 A narrative explanation **must** accompany each journal entry. It is required for audit and control, to indicate the purpose and authority of every transaction which is not first recorded in a book of prime entry.

**ASSESSMENT ALERT**

A question or simulation might ask you to 'journalise' transactions which are not in practice recorded in the journal. You should record the debit and credit entries for every transaction you can recognise, giving supporting narrative to each transaction.

### 3.4 EXAMPLE: JOURNAL ENTRIES

The following is a summary of the transactions of the Manon Beauty Salon of which David Blake is the sole proprietor.

| | |
|---|---|
| 1 October | Put in cash of £5,000 as capital<br>Purchased brushes, combs , clippers and scissors for cash of £485<br>Purchased hair driers from Juno Ltd on credit for £240 |
| 30 October | Paid three months rent to 31 December of £500<br>Collected and paid in to the bank takings of £1,000 |
| 31 October | Gave Mrs Sweet a perm and manicure on credit for £100. |

Show the transactions by means of journal entries.

## 3.5 SOLUTION

JOURNAL

| | | | £ | £ |
|---|---|---|---|---|
| 1 October | DEBIT | Cash | 5,000 | |
| | CREDIT | David Blake: capital account | | 5,000 |
| | *Initial capital introduced* | | | |
| 1 October | DEBIT | Brushes, combs and scissors account | 485 | |
| | CREDIT | Cash | | 485 |
| | *The purchase for cash of brushes etc as fixed assets* | | | |
| 1 October | DEBIT | Hair dryer account | 240 | |
| | CREDIT | Sundry creditors account * | | 240 |
| | *The purchase on credit of hair driers as fixed assets* | | | |
| 30 October | DEBIT | Rent account | 500 | |
| | CREDIT | Cash | | 500 |
| | *The payment of rent to 31 December* | | | |
| 30 October | DEBIT | Cash | 1,000 | |
| | CREDIT | Sales (or takings account) | | 1,000 |
| | *Cash takings* | | | |
| 31 October | DEBIT | Debtors account | 100 | |
| | CREDIT | Sales account (or takings account) | | 100 |
| | *The provision of a hair-do and manicure on credit* | | | |

**Note*. Creditors who have supplied fixed assets are included in **sundry creditors**, as distinct from creditors who have supplied raw materials or goods for resale, who are **trade creditors.**

### The correction of errors

3.6 The journal is most commonly used to record **corrections to errors that have been made** in writing up the general ledger accounts. Errors corrected by the journal **must be capable of correction by means of a double entry** in the ledger accounts. The error must not have caused total debits and total credits to be unequal.

### Journal vouchers

3.7 Journal entries might be logged, not in a single 'book' or journal, but on a separate slip of paper, called a **journal voucher**.

**KEY TERM**

A **journal voucher** is used to record the equivalent of one entry in the journal.

3.8 The use of journal vouchers is fairly widespread because:

(a) Certain journal entries are **repetitive** (vouchers can be pre-printed to standardise the narrative of such entries, and to save time in writing them out)

(b) A voucher is able to hold **more information** than a conventional journal record

## 4 THE INITIAL TRIAL BALANCE

4.1 There is no foolproof method for making sure that all entries have been posted to the correct ledger account, but a technique which shows up the more obvious mistakes is to prepare a **trial balance**.

**KEY TERM**

A **trial balance** is a list of ledger balances shown in debit and credit columns.

### Collecting together the ledger accounts

4.2 Before you draw up a trial balance, you must have a **collection of ledger accounts**. These are the ledger accounts of Shabnum Rashid, a sole trader.

CASH

| | £ | | £ |
|---|---|---|---|
| Capital: Shabnum Rashid | 10,000 | Rent | 4,200 |
| Bank loan | 3,000 | Shop fittings | 3,600 |
| Sales | 14,000 | Trade creditors | 7,000 |
| Debtors | 3,300 | Bank loan interest | 130 |
| | | Incidental expenses | 2,200 |
| | | Drawings | 1,800 |
| | | | 18,930 |
| | | Balancing figure: the amount of cash left over after payments have been made | 11,370 |
| | 30,300 | | 30,300 |

CAPITAL (SHABNUM RASHID)

| | £ | | £ |
|---|---|---|---|
| | | Cash | 10,000 |

BANK LOAN

| | £ | | £ |
|---|---|---|---|
| | | Cash | 3,000 |

PURCHASES

| | £ | | £ |
|---|---|---|---|
| Trade creditors | 7,000 | | |

TRADE CREDITORS

| | £ | | £ |
|---|---|---|---|
| Cash | 7,000 | Purchases | 7,000 |

RENT

| | £ | | £ |
|---|---|---|---|
| Cash | 4,200 | | |

SHOP FITTINGS

| | £ | | £ |
|---|---|---|---|
| Cash | 3,600 | | |

SALES

| | £ | | £ |
|---|---|---|---|
| | | Cash | 14,000 |
| | | Debtors | 3,300 |
| | | | 17,300 |

DEBTORS

| | £ | | £ |
|---|---|---|---|
| Sales | 3,300 | Cash | 3,300 |

BANK LOAN INTEREST

| | £ | | £ |
|---|---|---|---|
| Cash | 130 | | |

OTHER EXPENSES

| | £ | | £ |
|---|---|---|---|
| Cash | 2,200 | | |

DRAWINGS ACCOUNT

| | £ | | £ |
|---|---|---|---|
| Cash | 1,800 | | |

The first step is to **'balance' each account.**

## Balancing ledger accounts

4.3 At the end of an accounting period, a balance is struck on each account in turn. This means that all the **debits** on the account are totalled and so are all the **credits.**

- If the **total debits exceed the total credits** the account has a **debit balance.**
- If the **total credits exceed the total debits** then the account has a **credit balance.**

4.4 Let's see how this works with Shabnum Rashid's cash account.

***Step 1*** **Calculate a total** for **both sides** of **each ledger account.**

Dr £30,300, Cr £18,930

***Step 2*** **Deduct** the **lower** total **from** the **higher** total.

£(30,300 – 18,930) = £11,370

*Step 3* **Insert the result of Step 2 as the balance c/d** on the side of the account with the lower total. Here it will go on the credit side, because the total credits on the account are less than the total debits.

*Step 4* **Check** that the **totals on both sides** of the account are **now the same.**

Dr £30,300, Cr £(18,930 + 11,370) = £30,300

*Step 5* **Insert the amount of the balance c/d as the new balance b/d on the other side of the account.**

The new balance b/d is the balance on the account. The balance b/d on the account is £11,370 Dr.

4.5 In our simple example, there is very little balancing to do.

(a) Both the trade creditors account and the debtors account balance off to zero.
(b) The cash account has a debit balance (the new balance b/d) of £11,370 (see above).
(c) The total on the sales account is £17,300, which is a credit balance.

The other accounts have only one entry each, so there is no totalling to do.

## Collecting the balances on the ledger accounts

4.6 If the basic principle of double entry has been correctly applied throughout the period the **credit balances will equal the debit balances** in total. This is illustrated by collecting together the balances on Shabnum Rashid's accounts.

| | *Debit* | *Credit* |
|---|---|---|
| | £ | £ |
| Cash | 11,370 | |
| Capital | | 10,000 |
| Bank loan | | 3,000 |
| Purchases | 7,000 | |
| Trade creditors | - | - |
| Rent | 4,200 | |
| Shop fittings | 3,600 | |
| Sales | | 17,300 |
| Debtors | - | - |
| Bank loan interest | 130 | |
| Other expenses | 2,200 | |
| Drawings | 1,800 | |
| | 30,300 | 30,300 |

4.7 The order of the various accounts listed in the **trial balance** does not matter, it is not a document that a company *has* to prepare. It is just a method used to test the accuracy of the double entry bookkeeping.

## What if the trial balance shows unequal debit and credit balances?

4.8 If the trial balance does not **balance** there must be an **error in recording of transactions in the accounts.** A trial **balance** will **not** disclose the following types of errors.

| | |
|---|---|
| *Type 1* | The **complete omission** of a transaction, because neither a debit nor a credit is made. |
| *Type 2* | A posting to the correct side of the ledger, but to a **wrong account** (also called errors of commission). |
| *Type 3* | **Compensating errors** (eg debit error of £100 is cancelled by credit £100 error elsewhere). |
| *Type 4* | **Errors of principle** (eg cash received from debtors being debited to the debtors control account and credited to cash instead of the other way round). |

## 4.9 EXAMPLE: TRIAL BALANCE

As at the end of 29 November 20X1, your business High & Mighty has the following balances on its ledger accounts.

| *Accounts* | *Balance* £ |
|---|---|
| Bank loan | 15,000 |
| Cash | 13,080 |
| Capital | 11,000 |
| Rates | 2,000 |
| Trade creditors | 14,370 |
| Purchases | 16,200 |
| Sales | 18,900 |
| Sundry creditors | 2,310 |
| Debtors | 13,800 |
| Bank loan interest | 1,000 |
| Other expenses | 12,500 |
| Vehicles | 3,000 |

During 30 November the business made the following transactions.

(a) Bought materials for £1,400, half for cash and half on credit
(b) Made £1,610 sales, £1,050 of which were for credit
(c) Paid wages to shop assistants of £300 in cash

You are required to draw up a trial balance showing the balances as at the end of 30 November 20X1.

## 4.10 SOLUTION

**Step 1** Put the opening balances into a trial balance, so decide which are debit and which are credit balances.

| *Account* | *Debit* | *Credit* |
|---|---|---|
| | £ | £ |
| Bank loan | | 15,000 |
| Cash | 13,080 | |
| Capital | | 11,000 |
| Rates | 2,000 | |
| Trade creditors | | 14,370 |
| Purchases | 16,200 | |
| Sales | | 18,900 |
| Sundry creditors | | 2,310 |
| Debtors | 13,800 | |
| Bank loan interest | 1,000 | |
| Other expenses | 12,500 | |
| Vehicles | 3,000 | |
| | 61,580 | 61,580 |

**Step 2** Take account of the effects of the three transactions which took place on 30 November 20X1.

| | | | £ | £ |
|---|---|---|---|---|
| (a) | DEBIT | Purchases | 1,400 | |
| | CREDIT | Cash | | 700 |
| | | Trade creditors | | 700 |
| (b) | DEBIT | Cash | 560 | |
| | | Debtors | 1,050 | |
| | CREDIT | Sales | | 1,610 |
| (c) | DEBIT | Other expenses | 300 | |
| | CREDIT | Cash | | 300 |

**Step 3** Amend the trial balance for these entries.

HIGH & MIGHTY: TRIAL BALANCE AT 30 NOVEMBER 20X1

| | *12/11/20X1* | | *Transactions* | | *30/11/20X1* | |
|---|---|---|---|---|---|---|
| | DR | CR | DR | CR | DR | CR |
| Bank loan | | 15,000 | | | | 15,000 |
| Cash | 13,080 | | (b) 560 | 700 (a) | 12,640 | |
| Capital | | 11,000 | | 300 (c) | | 11,000 |
| Rates | 2,000 | | | | 2,000 | |
| Trade creditors | | 14,370 | | 700 (a) | | 15,070 |
| Purchases | 16,200 | | (a) 1,400 | | 17,600 | |
| Sales | | 18,900 | | 1,610 (b) | | 20,510 |
| Sundry creditors | | 2,310 | | | | 2,310 |
| Debtors | 13,800 | | (b) 1,050 | | 14,850 | |
| Bank loan interest | 1,000 | | | | 1,000 | |
| Other expenses | 12,500 | | (c) 300 | | 12,800 | |
| Vehicles | 3,000 | | | | 3,000 | |
| | 61,580 | 61,580 | 3,310 | 3,310 | 63,890 | 63,890 |

## Activity 3.2

Bailey Hughes started trading as a wholesale bookseller on 1 June 20X7 with a capital of £10,000 with which he opened a bank account for his business.

During June the following transactions took place.

| | | |
|---|---|---|
| June | 1 | Bought warehouse shelving for cash from Warehouse Fitters Ltd for £3,500 |
| | 2 | Purchased books on credit from Ransome House for £820 |
| | 4 | Sold books on credit to Waterhouses for £1,200 |
| | 9 | Purchased books on credit from Big, White for £450 |
| | 11 | Sold books on credit to Books & Co for £740 |
| | 13 | Paid cash sales of £310 from the warehouse shop intact into the bank |
| | 16 | Received cheque from Waterhouses in settlement of their account |
| | 17 | Purchased books on credit from RUP Ltd for £1,000 |
| | 18 | Sold books on credit to R S Jones for £500 |
| | 19 | Sent cheque to Ransome House in settlement of their account |
| | 20 | Paid rent of £300 by cheque |
| | 21 | Paid delivery expenses of £75 by cheque |
| | 24 | Received £350 from Books & Co on account |
| | 30 | Drew cheques for personal expenses of £270 and assistant's wages £400 |
| | 30 | Settled the account of Big, White |

**Tasks**

(a) Record the foregoing in appropriate books of original entry.
(b) Post the entries to the ledger accounts.
(c) Balance the ledger accounts where necessary.
(d) Extract a trial balance at 30 June 20X7.

## 5 COMPUTERISED SYSTEMS

5.1 So far we have looked at the way an accounting system is organised. You should note that all of the books of prime entry and the ledgers may be either **hand-written books** or **computer records.** Most businesses use computers, ranging from one **PC** to huge **mainframe computer systems.**

5.2 All computer activity can be divided into three processes.

| Areas | Activity |
|---|---|
| **Input** | Entering data from original documents |
| **Processing** | Entering up books and ledgers and generally sorting the input information |
| **Output** | Producing any report desired by the managers of the business, including financial statements |

## Activity 3.3

Your friend Lou Dight believes that computerised accounting systems are more trouble than they are worth because 'you never know what is going on inside that funny box'.

**Task**

Explain briefly why computers might be useful in accounting.

5.3 Computers and computing are covered in detail in your studies for Unit 20 **Working with Information Technology.**

## Batch processing and control totals

> **KEY TERM**
>
> **Batch processing:** similar transactions are gathered into batches, then sorted and processed by the computer.

5.4 Inputting individual invoices into a computer for processing (**transaction processing**), is time consuming and expensive. Invoices can be gathered into a **batch** and **input and processed all together**. Batches can vary in size, depending on the type and volume of transactions and on any limit imposed by the system on batch sizes.

> **KEY TERM**
>
> **Control totals** are used to ensure there are no errors when the batch is input. They are used to ensure the total value of transactions input is the same as that previously calculated.

5.5 Say a batch of 30 sales invoices has a manually calculated total value of £42,378.47. When the batch is input, the computer adds up the total value of the invoices and produces a total of £42,378.47. The control totals agree, therefore no further action is required.

5.6 If the control total does **not agree** then checks have to be carried out until the difference is found. An invoice might not have been entered or the manual total incorrectly calculated.

## Key learning points

- A **journal** is a record of unusual movements between accounts. The journal format is:

| | | Folio | £ | £ |
|---|---|---|---|---|
| Date | | | | |
| DEBIT | Account to be debited | | X | |
| CREDIT | Account to be credited | | | X |

*Narrative to explain the transaction*

- Balances on ledger accounts can be collected on a trial balance. The debit and credit balances should be equal.
- Computer accounting systems perform the same tasks at manual accounting systems, but they can cope with greater volumes of transactions and process them at a faster rate.

## Quick quiz

1 What is the double entry for goods sold on credit which are standard-rated for VAT and whose price excluding VAT is £100?

2 Why must a journal include a narrative explanation?

3 A journal can be used to correct errors which cause the total debits and credits to be unequal. True or false?

4 What is the other name for a trial balance?

5 If the total debits in an account exceed the total credits, will there be a debit or credit balance on the account?

6 What types of error will *not* be discovered by drawing up a trial balance?

7 What are the advantages of batch processing?

## Answers to quick quiz

1 *Debit* Trade debtors £117.50; *Credit* Sales £100.00; *Credit* VAT £17.50.

2 The narrative is required for audit and control, to show the purpose and authority of the transaction.

3 False. The error must be capable of correction by double entry.

4 The trial balance is also sometimes called the 'list of account balances'.

5 There will be a debit balance on the account.

6 There are four types, summarised as: complete omission; posted to wrong account; compensating errors; errors of principle.

7 Batch processing is faster than transaction processing and checks on input can be made using control totals.

# 4 Bank reconciliations

## This chapter contains



## Learning objectives

On completion of this chapter you will be able to:

- Check that details from the primary documentation are recorded in the cash book
- Ensure totals of balances of receipts and payments are correctly calculated
- Carry out bank reconciliation activities

### Performance criteria

| | |
|---|---|
| 3.1 | Details from the relevant primary documentation are recorded in the cash book |
| 3.1 | Totals of balances of receipts and payments are correctly calculated |
| 3.1 | Individual items on the bank statement and in the cash book are compared for accuracy |
| 3.1 | Discrepancies are identified and referred to the appropriate person |

### Range statement

| | |
|---|---|
| 3.1 | Primary documentation: credit transfer and standing order schedules |
| 3.2 | Control accounts: cash |

### Knowledge and understanding

- General bank services
- Form and function of banking documentation
- Identification of different types of errors

## 1 INTRODUCTION

1.1 By now you'll be familiar with the cash book. But this is a record of the amount of cash the business **thinks** it has in the bank.

1.2 You, too, may have an idea of what your bank balance should be. But then you get your bank statement, and the amount is rather different...

## 2 BANK RECONCILIATIONS

### Why is a bank reconciliation necessary?

**CENTRAL ASSESSMENT ALERT**

You may be asked to state what the reasons are for a bank reconciliation or what the differences between a bank statement balance and a cash book balance are likely to be.

2.1 Why might your own estimate of your bank balance be different from the amount shown on your bank statement? There are three common explanations.

| Cause of difference | Explanation |
|---|---|
| **Errors** | Errors in calculation, or in recording income and payments, are as likely to have been made by yourself as the bank. These **errors must be corrected**. |
| **Bank charges or bank interest** | The bank might deduct interest on an overdraft or charges for its services, which you are not informed about until you receive the bank statement. **These should be accounted for in your records**. |
| **Timing differences** | (a) **Cheques recorded as received** and paid-in but not yet 'cleared' and added to your account by the bank. Your own records show that some cash has been added to your account. But it has not yet been acknowledged by the bank, although it will be in a very short time when the cheques are eventually cleared. |
| | (b) **Payments made by cheque** and recorded, but not yet banked by payee. Even when it is banked, it takes a day or two for the banks to process it and for the money to be deducted from your account. |

**KEY TERM**

A **bank reconciliation** compares the balance of cash in the business's records to the balance held by the bank. Differences between the balance on the bank statement and the balance in the cash book will be errors or timing differences, and they must be identified and satisfactorily explained.

## 3 THE BANK STATEMENT

3.1 It is common practice for a business to issue a monthly **statement** to each credit customer, itemising:

- The **balance** the customer owed on his account **at the beginning** of the month
- **New debts** incurred by the customer during the month
- **Payments** made by the customer during the month
- The **balance** the customer owes on his account **at the end of the month**

**REMEMBER!**

If a customer has money in his account, **the bank owes him that money**, and the customer is therefore a **creditor** of the bank. (If you are in 'credit', you have money in your bank account.)

3.2 Suppose if a business has £8,000 cash in the bank. It will have a debit balance in its own cash book, but the bank statement, if it reconciles exactly with the cash book, will state that there is a credit balance of £8,000 in the bank's 'creditors account'. (The bank's records are a 'mirror image' of the customer's own records, with debits and credits reversed.)

## What does a bank statement look like?

3.3 An example of a bank statement is shown below; nearly all bank statements will look something like this.

**Southern Bank** CONFIDENTIAL

200 BROMFORD AVENUE
LONDON
E11 8TH

Account: ABC & CO.
4 THE MEWS
LONDON E4 2P2

SHEET NO 52 (d)

Telephone 20X2 020 8359 3100 Statement date 13 JUN 20X2 (a) Account no 9309823 (b)

| Date | Details | Withdrawals | Deposits | Balance (£) |
|---|---|---|---|---|
| (c) 11MAY | Balance from Sheet no. 51 (d) | | | (f) 787.58 |
| 14MAY | 000059 (g) | 216.81 | | 570.77 |
| 22MAY | 000058 | 157.37 | | 413.40 |
| 24MAY | 000060 | 22.00 | | 391.40 |
| 29MAY | LION INSURANCE DD (i) | 87.32 | | |
| | CATS238/ 948392093 DD | 1,140.10 | | |
| | LB HACKBETH CC SO (j) | 54.69 | | |
| | COUNTER CREDIT 101479 (h) | | 469.86 | |
| | INTEREST (l) | 9.32 | | |
| | CHARGES (k) | 30.00 | | 460.17 O/D |
| 13JUN | Balance to Sheet no. 53 | | | (f) 460.17 O/D |

(e) **Key** **SO** Standing Order **EC** Eurocheque **DV** Dividend **TR** Transfer **CC** Cash &/or Cheques **CP** Card Purchases Auto Withdrawals { **AC** Automated cash **DD** Direct Debit **PY** Payroll **OD** Overdrawn **Interest** - see over

3.4 We have discussed nearly all of the items which appear here in the earlier chapters on receipts and payments. The following points refer to the circled letters on the bank statement.

| Letter | Item | Explanation |
|---|---|---|
| (a) | **Statement date** | Only transactions which have passed through your account **up to this date** (and since the last statement date) will be shown on the statement. |
| (b) | **Account number** | This number is required on the statement, particularly if the bank's customer has **more than one account**. |
| (c) | **Date** | This shows the date any transaction **cleared** into or out of your account. You may have made the transaction earlier. |
| (d) | **Sheet number** | Each bank statement received will have a number. The numbers run in **sequential order**; this shows if a statement is missing. |
| (e) | **Key** | Not all bank statements will have a key to the abbreviations they use but it is helpful when one is provided. Note the following.<br>• **Dividends** can be paid directly into a bank account if the shareholder has instructed the company in which he holds shares to do so.<br>• **Automated cash** is a withdrawal from an automated teller machine - unusual for a business.<br>• **Card purchase** is a purchase by debit card, again unusual for a business. |
| (f) | **Balance** | Most statements show a balance as at the end of each day's transactions. |
| (g) | **Cheque numbers** | The number is the same as that which appears on the individual cheque. Numbers are necessary to help you to **identify items** on the statement: you could not do so if only the amount of the cheque appeared. |
| (h) | **Paying-in slip numbers** | The need for these numbers is the same as for cheques. |
| (i) | **Direct debit payments and receipts** | The **recipient** of the direct debit payment is usually identified, either in words or by an account number. |
| (j) | **Standing order payments and receipts** | Again, the recipient is identifiable. |
| (k) | **Charges** | Based on the **number of transactions** (cheques, receipts and so on) which have been processed through your account in a given period (usually a quarter). |
| (l) | **Interest** | Interest is charged on the amount of an **overdrawn balance** for the period it is overdrawn. |

## Activity 4.1

The bank statement of Gary Jones Trading Ltd for the month of February 20X7 is shown below.

**Task**

You are required to explain briefly the shaded items on the statement.

**Southern Bank** CONFIDENTIAL

Clapham Common Branch
Clapham Common
London SW6

Account: Gary Jones Trading Ltd
3 Barnes Street
Clapham SW6

SHEET NO 72

Telephone 020 7728 4213

20X7 Statement date 28 February 20X7 Account no 01140146

| Date | Details | | Withdrawals | Deposits | Balance (£) |
|---|---|---|---|---|---|
| | Balance brought forward | | | | 1,225.37 |
| 1 Feb | Cheque | 800120 | 420.00 | | 805.37 |
| 4 Feb | Cheque | 800119 | 135.40 | | 669.97 |
| 7 Feb | Bank giro credit | Pronto Motors | | 162.40 | |
| 7 Feb | Credit | | | 380.75 | |
| 7 Feb | BACS | 7492 | 124.20 | | 1,088.92 |
| 9 Feb | Cheque | 800121 | 824.70 | | 264.22 |
| 11 Feb | Cheque | 800122 | 323.25 | | 59.03 OD |
| 14 Feb | Credit | | | 522.70 | 463.67 |
| 19 Feb | Credit | | | 122.08 | 585.75 |
| 21 Feb | BACS | | 124.20 | | |
| 21 Feb | Direct debit | Swingate Ltd | 121.00 | | 340.55 |
| 23 Feb | Bank giro credit | Bord & Sons | | 194.60 | 535.15 |
| 25 Feb | Cheque | 800123 | 150.00 | | 385.15 |
| 27 Feb | Credit | | | 242.18 | 627.33 |
| 28 Feb | Bank charges | | 15.40 | | 611.93 |
| 28 Feb | Balance to Sheet no. | 73 | | | 611.93 |

# 4 HOW TO PERFORM A BANK RECONCILIATION

**CENTRAL ASSESSMENT ALERT**

The Chief Assessor has said that bank reconciliation **statements** are not assessable but 'bank reconciliation **activities**' are. However, it is impossible to perform the activities in question without knowing how the bank reconciliation works.

4.1 The **cash book and bank statement will rarely agree at a given date**. Several procedures should be followed to ensure that the reconciliation between them is performed correctly.

***Step 1*** Identify the cash book balance and the bank balance (from the bank statement) on the date to which you wish to reconcile.

***Step 2*** Add up the cash book for the period since the last reconciliation and identify and note any errors found.

*Step 3* Examine the bank statements for the same period and identify those items which appear on the bank statement but which have not been entered in the cash book.

- Standing orders and direct debits (into and out of the account)
- Dividend receipts from investments
- Bank charges and interest

Make a list of all those found.

*Step 4* Identify all reconciling items due to timing differences.

(a) Some cheque payments made by the business and entered in the cash book have not yet been presented to the bank, or 'cleared', and so do not yet appear on the bank statement. You should really mark off cheques in the cash book as they clear through the bank on a daily or weekly basis. In this way it will always be easy to identify unpresented cheques when you do a reconciliation.

(b) Cheques received, entered in the cash book and paid into the bank, but which have not yet been cleared and entered in the account by the bank, do not yet appear on the bank statement.

## What does a bank reconciliation look like?

4.2 ADJUSTED CASH BOOK BALANCE

| | £ | £ |
|---|---|---|
| Cash book balance brought down | | X |
| Add: correction of understatement | X | |
| receipts not entered in cash book (standing orders, direct debits) | X | |
| | | X |
| Less: correction of overstatement | X | |
| payments/charges not entered in cash book (standing orders, direct debits) | X | |
| | | (X) |
| Corrected cash book balance | | A |

| BANK RECONCILIATION | £ |
|---|---|
| Balance per bank statement | X |
| Add cheques paid in and recorded in the cash book but not yet credited to the account by the bank (**outstanding lodgements**) | X |
| Less cheques paid by the company but not yet presented to the company's bank for settlement (**unpresented cheques**) | (X) |
| Balance per cash book | A |

## 4.3 EXAMPLE: BANK RECONCILIATION

At 30 September 20X3 the debit balance in the cash book of Dotcom Ltd was £805.15. A bank statement on 30 September 20X3 showed Dotcom Ltd to be in credit by £1,112.30.

On investigation of the difference between the two sums, three things come to light.

(a) The cash book had been added up wrongly on the debit side; it should have been £90.00 more.

(b) Cheques paid in not yet credited by the bank amounted to £208.20.

(c) Cheques drawn not yet presented to the bank amounted to £425.35.

We need to show the correction to the cash book and show a statement reconciling the balance per the bank statement to the balance in the cash book.

## 4.4 SOLUTION

BANK RECONCILIATION 30.9.X3

| | £ | £ |
|---|---|---|
| Cash book balance brought down | | 805.15 |
| Add correction of adding up | | 90.00 |
| Corrected balance | | 895.15 |
| Balance per bank statement | | 1,112.30 |
| Add cheques paid in, recorded in the cash book, but not yet credited to the account by the bank | 208.20 | |
| Less cheques paid by the company but not yet presented to the company's bank for settlement | (425.35) | |
| | | (217.15) |
| Balance per cash book | | 895.15 |

4.5 The reconciling items noted here will often consist of several transactions which can either be listed on the face of the reconciliation or listed separately. In particular, there may be a **great many outstanding cheques** if this is a busy business account.

4.6 You can see here that the reconciliation falls into **two distinct steps**:

***Step 1*** Correct the cash book.

***Step 2*** Reconcile the bank balance to the corrected cash book balance.

### Activity 4.2

The cash book of Gary Jones Trading Ltd for February 20X7 is set out below.

CASH BOOK

| *Receipts* | | | *Payments* | | | |
|---|---|---|---|---|---|---|
| *Date* | *Details* | | *Date* | *Details* | *Cheq no* | |
| 20X7 | | £ | 20X7 | | | £ |
| 1/2 | Balance b/d | 1,089.97 | 1/2 | Rent | 800120 | 420.00 |
| 3/2 | Pronto Motors | 162.40 | 4/2 | R F Lessing | 800121 | 824.70 |
| 3/2 | Cash sales | 380.75 | 4/2 | Wages | BACS | 124.20 |
| 11/2 | Cash sales | 522.70 | 11/2 | British Gas plc | 800122 | 323.25 |
| 16/2 | Cash sales | 122.08 | 18/2 | D Waite | 800123 | 150.00 |
| 24/2 | Cash sales | 242.18 | 18/2 | Wages | BACS | 124.20 |
| 28/2 | Warley's Ltd | 342.50 | 23/2 | S Molesworth | 800124 | 207.05 |
| | | | 25/2 | Fogwell & Co | 800125 | 92.44 |
| | | | 28/2 | Balance c/d | | 596.74 |
| | | 2,862.58 | | | | 2,862.58 |
| | Balance b/d | 596.74 | | | | |

**Task**

Using the information from the bank statement (Activity 4.1), complete the cash book entries for the month. (The transactions to be entered are those which appear on the bank statement but are not to be found in the cash book as shown above.) You do not need to reproduce the whole of the cash book given above.

The following additional information is available. The difference between the opening bank balance at 1 February per the cash book of £1,089.97 and the opening balance at 1 February per the bank statement of £1,225.37 CR is explained by the cheque number 800119 for £135.40 which was recorded in the cash book in January and presented on 7 February.

### Activity 4.3

Prepare a bank reconciliation statement for Gary Jones Trading as at 28 February 20X7 using the information given in Activities 4.1 and 4.2.

## Timing and frequency of the bank reconciliation

4.7 When and how often a company's bank reconciliation is performed depends on several factors.

| Factor | Considerations |
|---|---|
| **Frequency and volume of transactions** | The more transactions there are, then the greater the likelihood of error. |
| **Other controls** | If there are very few checks on cash other than the reconciliation, then it should be performed quite often. (Other checks would include agreeing receipts to remittance advices.) |
| **Cash flow** | If the company has to keep a very close watch on its cash position then the reconciliation should be performed as often as the information on cash balances is required. Most companies do a reconciliation at the end of each month. But if a company is very close to its overdraft limit, then it might need to do a weekly reconciliation. |
| **Number of bank accounts** | If, for some reason, a company has several bank accounts, all used regularly, then it may be impractical, or even impossible, to perform reconciliations very often. |

### Activity 4.4

At your firm, Gemfix Engineering Ltd, a new trainee has been asked to prepare a bank reconciliation statement as at the end of October 20X7. At 31 October 20X7, the company's bank statement shows an overdrawn balance of £142.50 DR and the cash book shows a favourable balance of £24.13.

You are concerned that the trainee has been asked to prepare the statement without proper training for the task. The trainee prepares the schedule below and asks you to look over it.

| | £ |
|---|---|
| Balance per bank statement (overdrawn) | 142.50 |
| Overdraft interest on bank statement, not in cash book | 24.88 |
| Unpresented cheques (total) | 121.25 |
| Cheque paid in, not credited on bank statement | (290.00) |
| Error in cash book* | 27.00 |
| | 25.63 |
| Unexplained difference | (1.50) |
| Balance per cash book | 24.13 |

*Cheque issued for £136.00, shown as £163.00 in the cash book.

The trainee says that he was not able to reconcile the difference completely, but was pleased that he was able to 'get it down' to £1.50. He feels that there is no need to do any more work now since the difference remaining is so small. He suggests leaving the job on one side for a week or so in the hope that the necessary information will come to light during that period.

**Tasks**

(a) So that you can show the trainee how a bank reconciliation ought to be performed, prepare:

(i) A statement of adjustments to be made to the cash book balance
(ii) A corrected bank reconciliation statement as at 31 October 20X7

(b) Explain to the trainee why it is important to prepare bank reconciliations regularly and on time.

## Stopped cheques

4.8 When you have received a cheque and banked it but it has already been stopped by the drawer, then the bank will not process it.

(a) You have already written the receipt in your cash book, but now it must be taken out again.

(b) This can be shown in the cash book as a deduction from receipts or an addition to payments, whichever is easier.

4.9 If you have written a cheque to someone and then subsequently you stop it, you must remove the payment from the cash book. If the reversal of the entry is not carried out then it will appear as a reconciling item on the bank reconciliation.

## Out of date cheques

4.10 Banks consider cheques 'stale' after six months. Cheques which have been written but which have not been presented to the bank will continue to appear on a reconciliation month after month.

| | |
|---|---|
| ***Step 1*** | Every time the reconciliation is performed you should check whether the oldest outstanding cheques are over six months old. |
| ***Step 2*** | Cancel or 'write back' such cheques in the cash book; they will then cease to be reconciling items. |
| ***Step 3*** | Notify the bank to stop the cheque and as a precaution. |
| ***Step 4*** | Raise a new cheque. |

## 5 CENTRAL ASSESSMENT ACTIVITIES

5.1 The Chief Assessor has said that you will not be asked to perform a bank reconciliation, but to perform **bank reconciliation activities**. However, the type of bank reconciliation activity seen so far in the Specimen Simulation and Central Assessment tells you to:

> (a) Check items on the bank statement against the cash book and **update** the **cash book**
>
> (b) **Give reasons why** the balance in the updated cash book **does not match** the closing balance on the bank statement

5.2 The 'reasons' you will give are, in effect, the **reconciling items** that would appear in a bank reconciliation. This is why we have shown you how to do them. Now we will show you what you have to do in the assessment.

### 5.3 EXAMPLE: AAT STYLE BANK RECONCILIATION ACTIVITY

On 1 July, Spaced Ltd received the following bank statement as at 30 June 20X0, which you are to check against the cash book shown below.

(a) Check the items on the bank statement against the items in the cash book and update the cash book accordingly. Total the cash book and show clearly the balance carried down.

**EARTH BANK plc**

High Street, Little Wood, Manchester M72 1AD

To: Spaced Ltd Account No 46138291 30 November 20X0

**STATEMENT OF ACCOUNT**

| DATE | DETAILS | DEBIT | CREDIT | BALANCE |
|---|---|---|---|---|
| 20X0 | | £ | £ | £ |
| 1 June | Balance b/f | | | 2,626 C |
| 5 June | Cheque No 218465 | 58 | | 2,568 C |
| 5 June | Credit | | 580 | 3,148 C |
| 8 June | Bank Giro Credit | | | |
| | Space Dust | | 6,600 | 9,748 C |
| 10 June | Cheque No 218467 | 8,000 | | 1,748 C |
| 16 June | Direct debit | | | |
| | B A Williams Ltd | 1,400 | | 348 C |
| 24 June | Bank charges | 108 | | 240 C |
| 25 June | Direct debit | | | |
| | Land Security | 200 | | 40 C |
| 30 June | Cheque No 218468 | 540 | | 500 D |

D = Debit C = Credit

**CASH BOOK**

| Date 20X0 | Details | Bank £ | Date 20X0 | Cheque No | Details | Bank £ |
|---|---|---|---|---|---|---|
| 1 June | Balance b/f | 2,626 | 1 June | 218465 | Crosby & Co | 58 |
| 1 June | L Green | 580 | 5 June | 218466 | LTF Ltd | 470 |
| 24 June | B Brown | 2,350 | 12 June | 218467 | P&S Insurance | 8,000 |
| 25 June | C Black | 7,990 | 23 June | 218468 | Derby & White | 540 |
| | | | 29 June | 218469 | The Space Pod | 705 |

(b) Using the above data, give FOUR reasons why the balance in your updated cash book does not match the closing balance on the bank statement.

1 ..........

2 ..........

3 ..........

4 ..........

## 5.4 SOLUTION

(a)

**CASH BOOK**

| Date 20X0 | Details | Bank £ | Date 20X0 | Cheque No | Details | Bank £ |
|---|---|---|---|---|---|---|
| 1 June | Balance b/f | 2,626 | 1 June | 218465 | Crosby & Co | 58 |
| 1 June | L Green | 580 | 5 June | 218466 | LTF Ltd | 470 |
| 24 June | B Brown | 2,350 | 12 June | 218467 | P&S Insurance | 8,000 |
| 25 June | C Black | 7,990 | 23 June | 218468 | Derby & White | 540 |
| 8 June | Space Dust | 6,600 | 29 June | 218469 | The Space Pod | 705 |
| | | | 16 June | DD | B A Williams | 1,400 |
| | | | 24 June | DD | Bank charges | 108 |
| | | | 25 June | DD | Land Security | 200 |
| | | | | | Balance c/d | 8,665 |
| | | 20,146 | | | | 20,146 |
| 1 July | Balance b/d | 8,665 | | | | |

(b) 1 Unpresented cheque to LTF Ltd for £470

2 Unpresented cheque to the Space Pod for £705

3 Uncleared deposit from B Brown: £2,350

4 Uncleared deposit from C Black: £7,990

*Note.* For information, you can check that you have got part (a) right by doing a mini bank reconciliation.

| | £ |
|---|---|
| **Balance per bank statement** | (500) |
| **Unpresented cheques (470 + 705)** | (1,175) |
| | (1,675) |
| **Uncleared deposits (2,350 + 7,990)** | 10,340 |
| **Balance per cash book** | 8,665 |

However, this will not be required in an assessment.

5.5 Now have a go at an AAT style activity yourself.

## Activity 4.5

On 1 October 20X0, Talbot Windows received a bank statement relating to the month of September 20X0.

(a) Update the cash book, checking items against the bank statement. Total the cash book, showing clearly the balance carried down.

(b) Give three reasons why the balance in the cash book does not agree with the balance on the bank statement.

**WEST BANK plc**
220 High Street, Bolton, BL9 4BQ

To: Talbot Windows Account No 48104039 30 September 20X0

**STATEMENT OF ACCOUNT**

| DATE | DETAILS | DEBIT | CREDIT | BALANCE |
|---|---|---|---|---|
| 20X0 | | £ | £ | £ |
| 1 Sept | Balance b/f | | | 13,400 |
| 4 Sept | Cheque No 108300 | 1,200 | | 12,200 |
| 1 Sept | Counter credit | | 400 | 12,600 |
| 8 Sept | Credit transfer | | | |
| | Zebra Sales | | 4,000 | 16,600 |
| 10 Sept | Cheque No 108301 | 470 | | 16,130 |
| 16 Sept | Standing order | | | |
| | West Council | 300 | | 15,830 |
| 24 Sept | Bank charges | 132 | | 15,698 |
| 25 Sept | Standing order | | | |
| | Any Bank | 400 | | 15,298 |
| 30 Sept | Cheque No 108303 | 160 | | 15,138 |
| 30 Sept | Credit transfer | | | |
| | Bristol Ltd | | 2,000 | 17,138 |
| 30 Sept | Salaries | 9,024 | | 8,114 |

**CASH BOOK**

| Date 20X0 | Details | Bank £ | Date 20X0 | Cheque No | Details | Bank £ |
|---|---|---|---|---|---|---|
| 1 Sept | Balance b/f | 13,400 | 1 Sept | 108300 | J Hibbert | 1,200 |
| 1 Sept | L Peters | 400 | 5 Sept | 108301 | Cleanglass | 470 |
| 28 Sept | John Smith | 2,400 | 25 Sept | 108302 | Denham Insurers | 630 |
| 29 Sept | KKG Ltd | 144 | 29 Sept | 108303 | Kelvin Ltd | 160 |
| | | | | | Salaries | 9,024 |

**Reasons why the Cash Book Balance differs from the Bank Statement**

1 ..........................................................................................

2 ..........................................................................................

3 ..........................................................................................

4 ..........................................................................................

## 6 RECONCILIATIONS ON A COMPUTERISED SYSTEM

6.1 In essence there is **no difference between reconciling a manual cash book and reconciling a computerised cash book.**

### Computer controls over cash

6.2 In theory many of the same errors could occur in a computerised cash book as in a manual one. However, the computer will have **programme controls** built in to prevent or detect many of the errors.

| Error | Programme control |
|---|---|
| **Casting** | Computers are programmed to add up correctly. |
| **Updating from ledgers** | When money is received from debtors, it will be posted to the sales ledger. The computer will then automatically update the bank account in the nominal ledger. This means that receipts and payments are unlikely to be confused. |
| **Combined computer and manual cash books** | The manual cash book reflects transactions generated by the computer system (for instance cheque payments from the purchase ledger), and also transactions initiated outside the computer system ('one-off' events such as the purchase of capital assets). The manual transactions will also be entered on to the computer. When a bank reconciliation is due to take place, the first job might be to make sure that the computer bank account and the cash book balances agree. |

## 7 BANK SERVICES AND TYPES OF ACCOUNT

### Competition

7.1 Competition is fierce in the financial services industry. Banks must now compete against other kinds of financial institutions, such as building societies, for their business. As a result, the **range of services** and **types of account** offered to both personal and business customers has expanded as each institution fights for market share.

### Types of account

7.2 There are different types of account offered by all the different banks and building societies. The majority of them fall into one of these categories.

- Current account
- Deposit account
- Savings account
- Loan account
- Mortgage

All these accounts may be offered on different terms by different institutions, but they all offer a trade-off between:

- Minimum/maximum investment
- Charges/level of interest receivable or payable
- Withdrawal with or without penalties
- Minimum/maximum investment period
- Security required
- Maximum payment period (for loans/mortgage)

With such a wide range of accounts on offer, people can find the account which most suits their needs. It is worth visiting your local bank and building society offices and reading their literature on all the different accounts they offer.

### Business accounts

7.3 The majority of businesses will only run a **current account**. Deposit accounts are also available for businesses as business current accounts will **not usually** pay interest if the balance is in credit.

7.4 If a business has excess cash for a certain period of time, then it may put the money on **short term deposit on the money market** to earn some interest.

### Foreign exchange and related services

7.5 A **personal customer** will need various foreign exchange services, many of which you may have encountered.

7.6 A business customer will have a very different requirement for foreign exchange services from a bank. Some of the services for both importers and exporters are highly specialised and we will not consider them in too much detail. The main services supplied will be:

- Foreign exchange
- Handling payments from buyers to suppliers
- The provision of finance
- The provision of information to exporters

## Other services

7.7 Banks offer other services to business clients; the main ones are listed here.

| Name of service | Nature of service |
|---|---|
| **Safe custody services** | Valuables, including deeds or share certificates, can be held in the vaults of the bank. |
| **Insurance services** | These might include insuring the business's buildings. |
| **Business finance services** | (a) **Discounting** and **factoring** involves administering the client's debts.<br>(b) **Leasing** and **hire purchase** are forms of rental which help clients to buy large assets. |
| **Home banking** | Customers can control their banking needs from their own home or office by being connected directly to the bank's computer:<br>(a) Using a television and telephone link<br>(b) Using a computer<br>This service is very useful for those who are either housebound or need constant access to their accounts but have no time to contact their bank personally. |
| **CHAPS** | This stands for **Clearing House Automated Payment System**. It was introduced to allow the clearing banks to transmit high value, guaranteed, sterling payments for same day settlement. This can only be done by computer. Security procedures are rigorous. |
| **Pensions** | Most banks now offer advice on pensions, for both directors and employees. |

## Key learning points

- A **bank reconciliation** is a comparison between the bank balance recorded in the books of a business and the balance appearing on the bank statement.
- The comparison may reveal **errors** or **omissions** in the records of the business, which should be corrected by appropriate adjustments in the cash book.
- Once the cash book has been corrected it should be possible to reconcile its balance with the bank statement balance by taking account of **timing differences**: payments made and cheques received which are recorded in the cash book but have not yet cleared through the bank account and have not, therefore, appeared on the bank statement.
- Banks offer a **wide range of services**, only some of which are relevant to the business customer.

## Quick quiz

1 What are the three main reasons why a business's cash book balance might differ from the balance on a bank statement?

2 What is a bank reconciliation?

3 What is a bank statement?

4 Why are cheque numbers shown on the bank statement?

5 What are the two parts of a bank reconciliation statement?

6 Do business bank accounts usually pay interest?

## Answers to quick quiz

1 Reasons for disagreement are: errors; bank charges or interest; timing differences (for amounts to clear).

2 A bank reconciliation compares the balance of cash in the business's records to the balance held by the bank.

3 A bank statement is a document sent by a bank to its short-term debtor and creditor customers, itemising transactions over a certain period.

4 Cheque numbers aid identification of the transaction; the amount only would not be enough.

5 (a) The adjustment of the cash book balance.
(b) The reconciliation of the cash book balance to the bank statement.

*Note.* The AAT will not ask for a statement for (b), but will ask you for reasons for the difference between the adjusted cash book balance and the balance on the bank statement.

6 Business bank accounts do not usually pay interest, but it depends on the individual business's arrangement with the bank.

# *Part B*

# *Control accounts*

# 5 Stocks and bad debts

**This chapter contains**



**Learning objectives**

On completion of this chapter you will be able to:

- Understand the stock control account and reconcile any differences
- Complete petty cash and wages control accounts
- Account for bad and doubtful debts

**Performance criteria**

3.2 Relevant accounts are totalled

3.2 Appropriate adjustments are correctly processed and documented

**Range statement**

3.2.2 Control accounts: stock, wages, cash

3.2.3 Adjustments: to correct errors; to write off bad debts

**Knowledge and understanding**

- Inter-relationship of accounts – double entry system
- Methods of closing off ledger accounts
- Relevant understanding of the organisation's accounting systems and administrative systems and procedures

# 1 INTRODUCTION

1.1 The control accounts you will come across most frequently are for debtors and creditors. This chapter deals with the remaining control accounts which may come up in a central or devolved assessment: stock, petty cash and wages.

**ASSESSMENT ALERT**

Petty cash and wages were covered in detail in Units 1 and 2, so only a quick revision is needed here.

# 2 STOCK CONTROL ACCOUNTS

## What is a stock control account?

2.1 Stock is an important asset of the business. As such it will appear in the balance sheet. In addition, it is used to calculate the profit made by a business.

**KEY TERM**

The **stock control account** (also called the stock account) is used to record the value of stock that a business holds for resale.

2.2 The stock control account acts as a **totals account** for the subsidiary accounts which are records of each item of stock. This is best shown in a diagram.

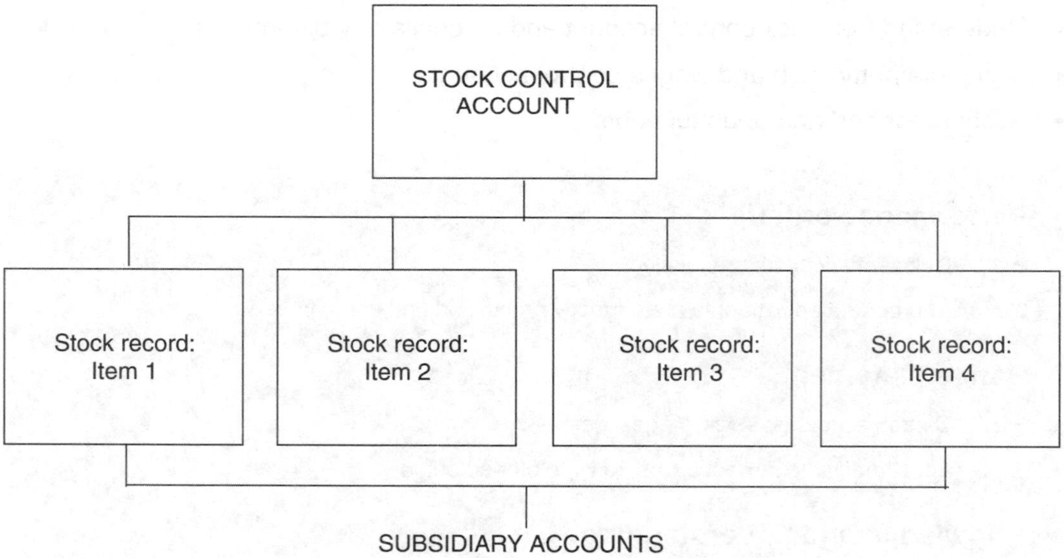


**REMEMBER!**

This stock account is only ever used at the end of an accounting period when the business counts up and values the stock in a physical stocktake.

2.3 At the end of the accounting period, the total of the individual stock records is entered in the stock control account. At the same time the stock is physically counted in a **stocktake** and valued. Stocktaking and the valuation techniques will be covered in your Intermediate studies.

2.4 The figure from the physical stocktake should **agree** with the future in the stock control account.

2.5 Any **differences** should be **investigated** and either resolved or referred to an appropriate person such as your supervisor.

## 2.6 TYPICAL QUESTION: STOCK CONTROL ACCOUNT

**STOCK CONTROL**

| Date | Details | £ | Date | Details | £ |
|---|---|---|---|---|---|
| 1 March | Balance b/f | 20,000 | | | |

This is the stock control account of XYZ Ltd. However, a recent physical stock check revealed goods in stock totalled £19,600. What may have caused this difference to occur?

## 2.7 SOLUTION

- Calculation  error in stock record
- Error in physical count of stock
- Error in stock receipt entry on stock record
- Damaged stock
- Theft

**ASSESSMENT ALERT**

The Chief Assessor for Unit 3 has said that this type of question would be typical. You could also be asked this without being given a control account.

In a simulation you may also be asked to complete a stock record card. This happened in the Specimen Simulation and is discussed below.

### Stock record cards

2.8 Businesses generally maintain **stock record cards** also known as 'stores record cards'.

2.9 Details from goods received notes and materials requisition notes or despatch notes are used to update the cards. The cards then provide a record of the quantity and value of each line of stock in the stores. These are the subsidiary records referred in Paragraph 2.2.

2.10 Here is an example of a stock record card.

STOCK RECORD CARD – B682 BALDWIN SEWING MACHINES

| Date | Details | In | Out | Quantity in stock | @ £100 per machine £ |
|---|---|---|---|---|---|
| 1 Jan | Opening balance | | | 200 | 20,000 |
| 6 Jan | Sales | | 10 | 190 | 19,000 |
| 10 Jan | Sales | | 30 | 160 | 16,000 |
| 15 Jan | Sales | | 20 | 140 | 14,000 |
| 17 Jan | Receipt | 40 | | 180 | 18,000 |
| 22 Jan | Sales | | 15 | 165 | 16,500 |
| 25 Jan | Sales | | 15 | 150 | 15,000 |
| 28 Jan | Receipt | 50 | | 200 | 20,000 |
| 31 Jan | Sales | | 10 | 190 | 19,000 |

2.11 **The balance on the stores record card may not agree with the level reported in a physical stocktake of the item. In a simulation or Central Assessment you may be asked to explain why. Have a go at this activity.**

### Activity 5.1

Suntime Ltd is a wholesaler of tanning equipment and beauty products. The year end is 31 December 20X1. A physical stock check has been carried out on product SB 248, the 'Rapidtan' sunbed. This revealed a stock of 139 items valued at £69,500.

### Task

Complete the stores record card below and reconcile with the stock check figure. If there is a difference, make a note to your supervisor, saying what you think is the reason for this.

**STOCK RECORD CARD – SB 248 RAPIDTAN SUNBEDS**

| Date 20X0 | Details | In | Out | Quantity in stock | @ £500 per sunbed £ |
|---|---|---|---|---|---|
| 1 Jan | Opening balance | | | 174 | 87,000 |
| 1 Jan | Sales | | 10 | 164 | 82,000 |
| 4 Jan | Sales | | 20 | 144 | 72,000 |
| 6 Jan | Sales | | 50 | 94 | 47,000 |
| 7 Jan | Sales | | 15 | | |
| 11 Jan | Sales | | 20 | | |
| 12 Jan | Faulty | | 1 | | |
| 13 Jan | Sales | | 20 | | |
| 15 Jan | Sales | | 20 | | |
| 18 Jan | Receipt | 100 | | | |
| 20 Jan | Sales | | 10 | | |
| 22 Jan | Sales | | 5 | | |
| 25 Jan | Sales | | 15 | | |
| 26 Jan | Sales | | 20 | | |
| 28 Jan | Receipt | 110 | | | |
| 29 Jan | Sales | | 20 | | |
| 30 Jan | Sales | | 20 | | |

**RECONCILIATION OF STOCK RECORD WITH PHYSICAL STOCK CHECK ON 31 JANUARY 20X0**

| | |
|---|---|
| PHYSICAL STOCK CHECK 139 @ £500 | ________ |
| STORES RECORD CARD QUANTITY | ________ |
| DIFFERENCE | ________ |

**NOTE FOR SUPERVISOR**

## 3 OTHER CONTROL ACCOUNTS

### Wages

3.1 You have covered this as part of your Unit 2 studies. For a quick revision, try this activity.

### Activity 5.2

The payroll clerk of Clegg Ltd has produced the following wages summary, which relates to June 20X1

**WAGES SUMMARY**

| | £ |
|---|---:|
| Gross wages | 8,600 |
| Net wages | 6,140 |
| Employer's NIC | 1,000 |
| Employees' NIC | 820 |
| Trade Union fees | 140 |
| PAYE | 1,500 |

### Task

Make the entries in the wages control account below and total it.

**WAGES CONTROL**

| Date 20X1 | Details | £ | Date 20X1 | Details | £ |
|---|---|---|---|---|---|
| | | | | | |

## Petty cash

3.2 You have covered petty cash payments and receipts in your studies for Units 1 and 2. A **cash control account** may be used with the petty cash book. In this case, the subsidiary account is the petty cash book.

3.3 A cash control account might look like this.

**CASH CONTROL ACCOUNT**

| Date 20X1 | Details | £ | Date 20X1 | Details | £ |
|---|---|---|---|---|---|
| 6 June | Balance b/d | 100.00 | 12 June | Petty cash book (Note) | 76.42 |
| 12 June | Bank | 76.42 | 12 June | Balance c/d | 100.00 |
| | | 176.42 | | | 176.42 |
| 13 June | Balance b/d | 100.00 | | | |

*Note.* £76.42 is the total of the analysis columns for the week. A transfer of £76.42 from the bank account is needed to restore the imprest amount to £100.

3.4 The cash control account forms **part of the double entry**. It should be agreed to the petty cash book (the subsidiary account) at regular intervals. Any discrepancies need to be investigated and either resolved or referred to your supervisor.

3.5 To make sure you have understood the cash control account, try this activity.

## Activity 5.3

A petty cash control account is kept in the main (general ) ledger of Astbury Ltd. The petty cash book is the subsidiary account. At the beginning of August there is a balance brought forward of £214.

During June £196 was spent from petty cash, and at the end of the month, £200 was put into the petty cash box from the bank.

### Task

Enter these transactions into the petty cash control account below, showing clearly the balance carried down.

**PETTY CASH CONTROL ACCOUNT**

| Date 20X1 | Details | £ | Date 20X1 | Details | £ |
|---|---|---|---|---|---|
| | | | | | |

## 4 BAD AND DOUBTFUL DEBTS

4.1 For some debts on the ledger, there may be little or no prospect of the business being paid.

- The customer has gone **bankrupt** .
- The customer is **out of business.**
- **Dishonesty** may be involved.

4.2 For one reason or another, therefore, a business might decide to give up expecting payment and to **write the debt off as a 'lost cause'**.

### Bad debts written off: ledger accounting entries

4.3 For bad debts written off, there is a **bad debts account** in the general ledger. The double-entry bookkeeping is fairly straightforward. When it is decided that a particular debt will not be paid, the customer is no longer called an outstanding debtor, and becomes a bad debt. We therefore:

| | | | |
|---|---|---|---|
| DEBIT | Bad debts account (expense) | £100 | |
| CREDIT | Debtors control account | | £100 |

**A write off of any bad debt will need the authorisation of a senior official in the organisation.**

### 4.4 EXAMPLE: BAD DEBTS WRITTEN OFF

At 1 October 20X1 a business had total outstanding debts of £8,600. During the year to 30 September 20X2:

(a) Credit sales amounted to £44,000.

(b) Payments from various debtors amounted to £49,000.

(c) Two debts, for £180 and £420 (both including VAT) were declared bad. These are to be written off.

We need to prepare the debtors control account and the bad debts account for the year.

## 4.5 SOLUTION

DEBTORS CONTROL ACCOUNT

| *Date* | *Details* | £ | *Date* | *Details* | £ |
|---|---|---|---|---|---|
| 1.10.X1 | Balance b/d | 8,600 | | Cash | 49,000 |
| | Sales for the year | 44,000 | 30.9.X2 | Bad debts | 180 |
| | | | 30.9.X2 | Bad debts | 420 |
| | | | 30.9.X2 | Balance c/d | 3,000 |
| | | 52,600 | | | 52,600 |
| | Balance b/d | 3,000 | | | |

BAD DEBTS

| *Date* | *Details* | £ | *Date* | *Details* | £ |
|---|---|---|---|---|---|
| 30.9.X2 | Debtors | 180 | 30.9.X2 | Balance | 600 |
| 30.9.X2 | Debtors | 420 | | | |
| | | 600 | | | 600 |

4.6 In the sales ledger, personal accounts of the customers whose debts are bad will be **taken off the ledger**. The business should then take steps to ensure that it does not sell goods to those customers again.

### Bad debts and VAT

4.7 A business can claim relief from VAT on bad debts which:

- Are **at least six months old** (from the time of supply)
- Which have been **written off** in the accounts of the business

4.8 VAT bad debt relief is accounted for as follows:

| | | | |
|---|---|---|---|
| DEBIT | VAT account | £17.50 | |
| | Bad debts | £100.00 | |
| CREDIT | Debtors control | | £117.50 |

## 4.9 EXAMPLE: BAD DEBTS AND VAT

If both the debts written off in the example above were inclusive of VAT, the accounts would look as follows:

DEBTORS CONTROL ACCOUNT - no change

BAD DEBTS

| *Date* | *Details* | £ | *Date* | *Details* | £ |
|---|---|---|---|---|---|
| 30.9.X2 | Debtors | 153.19 | 30.9.X2 | Balance | 510.64 |
| 30.9.X2 | Debtors | 357.45 | | | |
| | | 510.64 | | | 510.64 |

VAT ACCOUNT (part)

| *Date* | *Details* | £ | *Date* | *Details* | £ |
|---|---|---|---|---|---|
| 30.9.X2 | Debtors | 26.81 | | | |
| 30.9.X2 | Debtors | 62.55 | | | |

## Provision for doubtful debts: ledger accounting entries

4.10 A provision for doubtful debts is rather different from a bad debt written off. A business might know from past experience that, say, 2% of debtors' balances are unlikely to be collected. It would then be considered prudent to make a **general provision of 2% of total debtor balances.**

4.11 It may be that no particular customers are regarded as suspect and so it is not possible to write off any individual customer balances as bad debts.

4.12 The procedure is then to leave the total debtors account completely untouched, but to open up a provision account by the following entries:

| | | | |
|---|---|---|---|
| DEBIT | Doubtful debts account (expense) | £250 | |
| CREDIT | Provision for doubtful debts | | £250 |

When giving a figure for debtors, the credit balance on the provision account is deducted from the debit balance on total debtors.

4.13 In **subsequent** years, adjustments may be needed to the amount of the provision. The procedure to be followed then is as follows.

*Step 1* Calculate the **new provision** required.

*Step 2* Compare it with the **existing balance** on the provision account (ie the balance b/f from the previous accounting period).

*Step 3* Calculate the **increase or decrease** required.

(i) If a higher provision is required now (either because the total of debtors has increased, or because the percentage of total debtors which are doubtful has increased, or both):

*Step 3 (cont.)*

| | | | |
|---|---|---|---|
| DEBIT | Doubtful debts account (expense) | £50 | |
| CREDIT | Provision for doubtful debts | | £50 |

with the amount of the increase.

(ii) If a lower provision is needed now than before (either because the total of debtors has decreased, or because the percentage of total debtors which are doubtful has decreased, or both):

| | | | |
|---|---|---|---|
| DEBIT | Provision for doubtful debts | £75 | |
| CREDIT | Doubtful debts account (expense) | | £75 |

with the amount of the decrease.

## 4.14 EXAMPLE: PROVISION FOR DOUBTFUL DEBTS

John Seager has total debtors' balances outstanding at 31 December 20X3 of £28,000. He believes that about 1% of these balances will not be paid and wishes to make an appropriate provision. Before now, he has not made any provision for doubtful debts at all.

On 31 December 20X4 his debtors' balances amount to £40,000. His experience during the year has convinced him that a provision of 5% should be made.

What accounting entries should John make on 31 December 20X3 and 31 December 20X4, and what will be his net figure for debtors at those dates?

## 4.15 SOLUTION

*At 31 December 20X3*

Provision required = 1% × £28,000
= £280

Alex will make the following entries.

| | | | |
|---|---|---|---|
| DEBIT | Doubtful debts account | £280 | |
| CREDIT | Provision for doubtful debts | | £280 |

The net debtors figure will be:

| | £ |
|---|---|
| Sales ledger balances | 28,000 |
| Less provision for doubtful debts | 280 |
| | 27,720 |

*At 31 December 20X4*

Following the procedure described above, John will calculate:

| | £ |
|---|---|
| Provision required now (5% × £40,000) | 2,000 |
| Existing provision | (280) |
| Additional provision required | 1,720 |

| | | | |
|---|---|---|---|
| DEBIT | Doubtful debts account | £1,720 | |
| CREDIT | Provision for doubtful debts | | £1,720 |

The provision account will by now appear:

PROVISION FOR DOUBTFUL DEBTS

| *Date* | *Details* | £ | *Date* | *Details* | £ |
|---|---|---|---|---|---|
| 20X3 | | | 20X3 | | |
| 31 Dec | Balance c/d | 280 | 31 Dec | Doubtful debts account | 280 |
| 20X4 | | | 20X4 | | |
| 31 Dec | Balance c/d | 2,000 | 1 Jan | Balance b/d | 280 |
| | | | 31 Dec | Doubtful debts account | 1,720 |
| | | 2,000 | | | 2,000 |
| | | | 20X5 | | |
| | | | 1 Jan | Balance b/d | 2,000 |

Net debtors will be:

| | £ |
|---|---|
| Sales ledger balances/total debtors account | 40,000 |
| Less provision for doubtful debts | 2,000 |
| | 38,000 |

*Doubtful debts and VAT*

4.16 Because it is a general provision, the **provision for doubtful debts has no effect whatsoever on VAT.**

## Activity 5.4

Gavin is a wholesaler and the following information relates to his accounting year ending 30 September 20X2.

(a) Goods are sold on credit terms, but some cash sales are also transacted.

(b) At 1 October 20X1 Gavin's trade debtors amounted to £30,000 against which he had set aside a provision for doubtful debts of 5%.

(c) On 15 January 20X2 Gavin was informed the Fall Ltd had gone into liquidation, owing him £2,000. This debt was outstanding from the previous year.

(d) Cash sales during the year totalled £46,800, whilst credit sales amounted to £187,800.

(e) £182,500 was received from trade debtors.

(f) Settlement discounts allowed to credit customers were £5,300.

(g) Apart from Fall Ltd's bad debt, other certain bad debts amounted to £3,500.

(h) Gavin intends to retain the provision for doubtful debts account at 5% of outstanding trade debtors as at the end of the year, and the necessary entry is to be made.

**Task**

Enter the above transactions in Gavin's ledger accounts and (apart from the cash and bank and profit and loss accounts) balance off the accounts and bring down the balances as at 1 October 20X2.

*Helping hand.* Treat settlement discounts in the same way as you treat cash to settle debtors.

## Key learning points

- A **stock control account** is kept which is only ever used at the end of an accounting period, when the business counts up and values stock in hand.
- **Stock record cards** are generally kept for individual stock lines.
- The quantity of stocks held at the year end is established by means of a physical count of stock in an annual **stocktaking** exercise, or by a 'continuous' stocktake.
- Other control accounts include **wages** and **petty cash.**
- Some debts may need to be written off as '**bad debts**' because there is no real prospect of them being paid. Alternatively or additionally, a **provision for doubtful debts** may be created.
- Rather than affecting individual customer balances, a **provision** for doubtful debts recognises the fact that ordinarily a certain **proportion** of all debts are unlikely to be collected.

## Quick quiz

1 When is a stock control account used?

2 Why might the stock value from the physical stocktake differ from the value in the control account?

3 What accounting entries in the VAT account should be made when the provision for doubtful debts is set up?

## Answers to quick quiz

1 A stock control account is only used at the end of the accounting period.

2
- Theft
- Damaged stock
- Calculation or counting errors
- Error in stock receipt entry on stock record

3 None - it is a general provision and does not affect VAT.

# 6 Debtors control account

## This chapter contains



## Learning objectives

On completion of this chapter you will be able to:

- Total and reconcile the debtors control account in the main ledger with the total of debtors' balances in the sales ledger
- Identify and deal with discrepancies arising from the reconciliation of the debtors control account

## Performance criteria

| | |
|---|---|
| 3.2 | Relevant accounts are totalled |
| 3.2 | Control accounts are reconciled with the totals of the balances in the subsidiary ledger, where appropriate |
| 3.2 | Authorised adjustments are correctly processed and documented |
| 3.2 | Discrepancies arising from the reconciliation of control accounts are either resolved or referred to the appropriate person |

## Range statement

| | |
|---|---|
| 3.2.1 | Ledgers: main ledger; sub-ledger; integrated ledger |
| 3.2.2 | Control accounts: debtors |
| 3.2.3 | Adjustments: to correct errors |

## Knowledge and understanding

- Identification of different types of error
- Relationship between the accounting system and the ledger
- Reconciling control accounts with memorandum accounts

# 1 INTRODUCTION

1.1 In Chapter 2 we saw that:

(a) Sales invoices and cash received are logged in a **day book** or onto some equivalent listing or computer file which serves a similar purpose

(b) Each invoice and cash receipt is posted **singly** to an appropriate personal account in the sales ledger

**But these personal accounts are for memorandum purposes only and do not form a part of the double entry system.**

1.2 To record these transactions in the **double entry system** we do not need to deal with each invoice singly. Instead, the day books can be totalled at convenient intervals (eg daily, weekly or monthly) and these total amounts are recorded in the main ledger. For sales invoices, this means an accounting entry is made as follows.

| | | | |
|---|---|---|---|
| DEBIT | Debtors control account | £1,000 | |
| CREDIT | Sales account(s) | | £825 |
| | VAT account | | £175 |

## 2 DEBTORS CONTROL ACCOUNT

**KEY TERM**

A **control account** is an account in which a record is kept of the total value of a number of similar but individual items.

- A debtors control account is an account in which records are kept of transactions involving all debtors in total.
- The balance on the debtors control account at any time will represent the total amount due to the business at that time from its debtors.

2.1 A **control account is an (impersonal) ledger account which will appear in the main ledger.**

### Control accounts and personal accounts

2.2 The personal accounts of individual debtors are kept in the sales ledger, and the amount owed by each debtor will be a balance on that **debtor's personal account**. The amount owed by all the debtors together will be the balance on the **debtors control account**.

**REMEMBER!**

At any time the balance on the debtors control account should be equal to the sum of the individual balances on the personal accounts in the sales ledger.

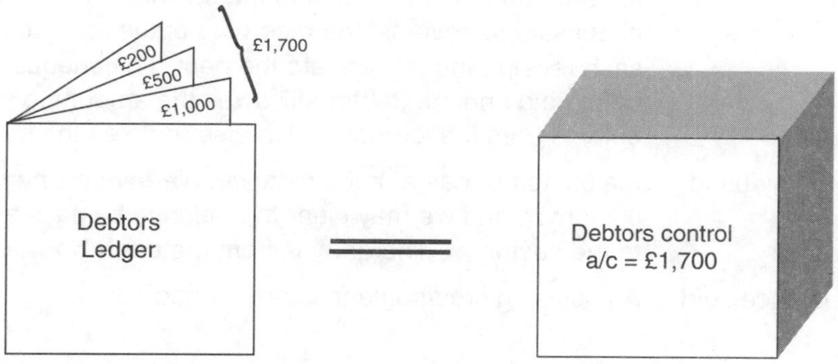


2.3 For example, if a business has three debtors, A Ashton who owes £80, B Bolton who owes £310 and C Collins who owes £200, the balances on the various accounts would be:

*Sales ledger (personal accounts)*

| | £ |
|---|---|
| A Ashton | 80 |
| B Bolton | 310 |
| C Collins | 200 |

All of these balances would be debit balances.

| | |
|---|---|
| *Main ledger: debtors control account* | 590 |

## 3 POSTING TO THE DEBTORS CONTROL ACCOUNT

3.1 Typical entries in a debtors control account are shown in the example below. The 'folio' reference 'Jnl' in this example indicates that the transaction is first **entered** in the **journal** before **posting** to the **control account** and other accounts indicated. The reference SDB is to the sales day book, the reference SRDB is to the sales returns day book and the reference CB is to the cash book.

DEBTORS CONTROL ACCOUNT

| | *Folio* | £ | | *Folio* | £ |
|---|---|---|---|---|---|
| Debit balances b/d | b/d | 7,000 | Credit balances c/d | b/d | 200 |
| Sales | SDB | 52,390 | Cash received | CB | 52,250 |
| Dishonoured cheques | Jnl | 1,000 | Discounts allowed | CB | 1,250 |
| Cash paid to clear credit balances | CB | 110 | Returns inwards from debtors | SRDB | 800 |
| Credit balances | c/d | 120 | Bad debts | Jnl | 300 |
| | | | Debit balances | c/d | 5,820 |
| | | 60,620 | | | 60,620 |
| Debit balances | b/d | 5,820 | Credit balances | b/d | 120 |

3.2 Note some points about the various kinds of entry shown above.

| **Debit entries** | **Points to note** |
|---|---|
| Debit balances b/d | Most **debtor balances** will be **debit balances**: customers will usually owe money to the business. |
| Sales | These are the **sales** totals posted periodically from the **sales day book**. The amounts recorded will include VAT, since debtors are due to pay the VAT to us. |
| Dishonoured cheques | A cheque received will be shown as a credit entry, since we treat it as **cash received**. If a cheque is dishonoured by the debtor's bank, it means that the cheque has 'bounced' and the amount will not be paid to the business. A **debit entry** is necessary to 'reverse' the recording of the cheque as a cash receipt and to reinstate the debt. The cheque has not been paid and the debtor still owes the amount to us. The entry is from the journal, which also updates the cash book. |
| Cash paid by us to clear credit balances | If a customer has a credit balance, **we owe money** to that customer, and we may clear the balance by paying money to the customer. The entry is from the **cash book.** |
| Credit balances c/d | Any closing credit balances are carried down. |

| **Credit entries** | **Points to note** |
|---|---|
| Credit balances b/d | **Credit balances** in the debtors control account can arise, for example, if goods which have already been paid for are **returned**, or if a customer has **overpaid**. Such balances will be unusual. |
| Cash received | **Cash received from debtors** will be posted from the **cash book.** |
| Discounts allowed | **Cash discounts allowed** may be recorded in a memorandum column in the cash book. They form a part of the amounts invoiced to customers which we are 'allowing' them not to pay, so a credit entry is needed to cancel that part of amounts invoiced which is being allowed as discount, posted from the **cash book**. |

| | |
|---|---|
| Returns inwards | **Credit notes** for returns inwards must be posted from the **sales returns day book**. |
| Bad debts | Bad debts written off need to be **cancelled** from the control account by means of a credit entry (debit bad debts account). Usually the source will be the **journal**. |
| Debit balances c/d | The bulk of sales ledger balances to carry forward will be debit balances. |

### Activity 6.1

Prepare a specimen sales ledger control account in T account form. Show clearly the information it would contain and the sources of this information.

### Activity 6.2

Tick the items below which you would **not** expect to see as individual items in a sales ledger control account.

1 Credit balances on individual debtor accounts
2 Debit balances on individual debtor accounts
3 Cash sales
4 Sales on credit
5 Provision for bad and doubtful debts
6 Settlement discounts allowed
7 Trade discounts received
8 Cash receipts
9 Bad debts written off
10 Sales returns
11 Credit notes received
12 Credit notes issued

### CENTRAL ASSESSMENT ALERT

You should learn this topic thoroughly as it is very likely to come up in a Central Assessment. Now we are ready for a comprehensive example!

## 4 COMPREHENSIVE EXAMPLE: ACCOUNTING FOR DEBTORS

4.1 This is a good point at which to go through the steps of how transactions involving debtors are **accounted for** in a comprehensive illustrative example (involving settlement discounts). Folio numbers are shown in the accounts to illustrate the cross-referencing that is needed and in the example folio numbers begin with either:

(a) SDB, referring to a page in the sales day book; or
(b) SL, referring to a particular account in the sales ledger; or
(c) GL, referring to a particular account in the main ledger; or
(d) CB, referring to a page in the cash book.

4.2 At 1 July 20X7, the Software Design Company had no debtors at all. During July, the following transactions affecting credit sales and customers occurred. All sales figures are gross; VAT on sales is charged at 17.5%.

- July 3 Invoiced A Ashton for the sale on credit of hardware goods: £100.

- July 11 Invoiced B Bolton for the sale on credit of electrical goods: £150.
- July 15 Invoiced C Collins for the sale on credit of hardware goods: £250.
- July 17 Invoiced D Derby for the sale on credit of hardware goods: £400. Goods invoiced at £120 were returned for full credit on the next day.
- July 10 Received payment from A Ashton of £100, in settlement of his debt in full.
- July 18 Received a payment of £80 from B Bolton.
- July 28 Received a payment of £120 from C Collins.
- July 29 Received a payment of £280 from D Derby.

Cash sales in July amounted to £2,502, all including VAT. £976 was for hardware goods, the balance for electrical.

Account numbers are as follows.

| | |
|---|---|
| SL4 | Personal account A Ashton |
| SL9 | Personal account B Bolton |
| SL13 | Personal account C Collins |
| SL21 | Personal account D Derby |
| GL6 | Debtors control account |
| GL21 | Sales - hardware |
| GL22 | Sales - electrical |
| GL1 | Cash account |
| GL2 | VAT account |

## 4.3 SOLUTION

The recording entries, suitably dated, would be as follows.

SALES DAY BOOK SDB35

| *Date* | *Name* | *Folio* | *Gross total* | *VAT* | *Net total* | *Hard-ware* | *Elect-rical* |
|---|---|---|---|---|---|---|---|
| 20X7 | | | £ | £ | £ | £ | £ |
| July 3 | A Ashton | SL4 Dr | 100.00 | 14.89 | 85.11 | 85.11 | |
| July 11 | B Bolton | SL9 Dr | 150.00 | 22.34 | 127.66 | | 127.66 |
| July 15 | C Collins | SL13 Dr | 250.00 | 37.23 | 212.77 | 212.77 | |
| July 17 | D Derby | SL21 Dr | 400.00 | 59.57 | 340.43 | 340.43 | |
| July 18 | D Derby | SL 21 Cr | (120.00) | (17.87) | (102.13) | (102.13) | |
| | | | 780.00 | 116.16 | 663.84 | 536.18 | 127.66 |
| | | | GL6 Dr | GL2 Cr | | GL21 Cr | GL22 Cr |

*Note*. The personal accounts in the sales ledger are debited on the day the invoices and credit notes are sent out. The double entry in the main ledger accounts might be made at the end of each day, week or month; here it is made at the end of the month, by posting from the sales day book as follows.

POSTING SUMMARY - SDB 35 31/7/X7

| | | *Debit* | *Credit* |
|---|---|---|---|
| | | £ | £ |
| GL 6 | Debtors control account | 780.00 | |
| GL21 | Sales - hardware | | 536.18 |
| GL22 | Sales - electrical | | 127.66 |
| GL2 | VAT | | 116.16 |

CASH BOOK EXTRACT
RECEIPTS - JULY 20X7

CB 23

| *Date* | *Name* | *Folio* | *Gross total* | *VAT* | *Net total* | *Debtors* | *Hard-ware* | *Elect-rical* |
|---|---|---|---|---|---|---|---|---|
| 20X7 | | | £ | £ | £ | £ | £ | £ |
| July 10 | A Ashton | SL4 Cr | 100.00 | | | 100.00 | | |
| July 18 | B Bolton | SL9 Cr | 80.00 | | | 80.00 | | |
| July 28 | C Collins | SL13 Cr | 120.00 | | | 120.00 | | |
| July 29 | D Derby | SL 21 Cr | 280.00 | | | 280.00 | | |
| July | Cash sales | | 2,502.00 | 372.64 | 2,129.36 | | 830.64 | 1,298.72 |
| | | | 3,082.00 | 372.64 | 2,129.36 | 580.00 | 830.64 | 1,298.72 |
| | | | GL1 Dr | GL2 Cr | | GL 6 Cr | GL21 Cr | GL22 Cr |

As with the sales day book, a posting summary to the main ledger needs to be drawn up for the cash book.

POSTING SUMMARY - CB 23 31/7/X7

| | | *Debit* | *Credit* |
|---|---|---|---|
| | | £ | £ |
| GL 1 | Cash account | 3,082.00 | |
| GL 6 | Debtors control account | | 580.00 |
| GL 21 | Sales – hardware | | 830.64 |
| GL 22 | Sales – electrical | | 1,298.72 |
| GL 2 | VAT | | 372.64 |

The personal accounts in the sales ledger are memorandum accounts, because they are not a part of the double entry system.

MEMORANDUM SALES LEDGER

A ASHTON — A/c no: SL4

| *Date* | *Narrative* | *Folio* | £ | *Date* | *Narrative* | *Folio* | £ |
|---|---|---|---|---|---|---|---|
| 20X7 | | | | 20X7 | | | |
| July 3 | Sales | SDB 35 | 100.00 | July 10 | Cash | CB 23 | 100.00 |
| | | | 100.00 | | | | 100.00 |

B BOLTON — A/c no: SL9

| *Date* | *Narrative* | *Folio* | £ | *Date* | *Narrative* | *Folio* | £ |
|---|---|---|---|---|---|---|---|
| 20X7 | | | | 20X7 | | | |
| July 11 | Sales | SDB 35 | 150.00 | July 18 | Cash | CB 23 | 80.00 |
| | | | | July 31 | Balance b/d | | 70.00 |
| | | | 150.00 | | | | 150.00 |
| Aug 1 | Balance b/d | | 70.00 | | | | |

C COLLINS — A/c no: SL13

| *Date* | *Narrative* | *Folio* | £ | *Date* | *Narrative* | *Folio* | £ |
|---|---|---|---|---|---|---|---|
| 20X7 | | | | 20X7 | | | |
| July 15 | Sales | SDB 35 | 250.00 | July 28 | Cash | CB 23 | 120.00 |
| | | | | July 31 | Balance c/d | | 130.00 |
| | | | 250.00 | | | | 250.00 |
| Aug 1 | Balance b/d | | 130.00 | | | | |

D DERBY — A/c no: SL21

| *Date* | *Narrative* | *Folio* | £ | *Date* | *Narrative* | *Folio* | £ |
|---|---|---|---|---|---|---|---|
| 20X7 | | | | 20X7 | | | |
| July 17 | Sales | SDB 35 | 400.00 | July 18 | Returns | SDB 35 | 120.00 |
| | | | | July 29 | Cash | CB 23 | 280.00 |
| | | | 400.00 | | | | 400.00 |

In the main ledger, the accounting entries can be made from the books of prime entry to the ledger accounts, in this example at the end of the month.

MAIN LEDGER (EXTRACT)

DEBTORS CONTROL ACCOUNT A/c no: GL6

| *Date* | *Narrative* | *Folio* | £ | *Date* | *Narrative* | *Folio* | £ |
|---|---|---|---|---|---|---|---|
| 20X7 | | | | 20X7 | | | |
| July 31 | Sales | SDB 35 | 780.00 | July 31 | Cash | CB 23 | 580.00 |
| | | | | | Balance c/d | | 200.00 |
| | | | 780.00 | | | | 780.00 |
| Aug 1 | Balance b/d | | 200.00 | | | | |

*Note*. At 31 July the closing balance on the debtors control account (£200) is the same as the total of the individual balances on the personal accounts in the sales ledger (£0 + £70 + £130 + £0).

VAT A/c no: GL 2

| *Date* | *Narrative* | *Folio* | £ | *Date* | *Narrative* | *Folio* | £ |
|---|---|---|---|---|---|---|---|
| 20X7 | | | | 20X7 | | | |
| | | | | July 31 | Debtors | SDB 35 | 116.16 |
| | | | | July 31 | Cash | CB 23 | 372.64 |

CASH ACCOUNT A/c no: GL1

| *Date* | *Narrative* | *Folio* | £ | *Date* | *Narrative* | *Folio* | £ |
|---|---|---|---|---|---|---|---|
| 20X7 | | | | | | | |
| July 31 | Cash received | CB 23 | 3,082.00 | | | | |

SALES - HARDWARE A/c no: GL21

| *Date* | *Narrative* | *Folio* | £ | *Date* | *Narrative* | *Folio* | £ |
|---|---|---|---|---|---|---|---|
| | | | | 20X7 | | | |
| | | | | July 31 | Debtors | SDB 35 | 536.18 |
| | | | | July 31 | Cash | CB 23 | 830.64 |

SALES - ELECTRICAL A/c no: GL22

| *Date* | *Narrative* | *Folio* | £ | *Date* | *Narrative* | *Folio* | £ |
|---|---|---|---|---|---|---|---|
| | | | | 20X7 | | | |
| | | | | July 31 | Debtors | SDB 35 | 127.66 |
| | | | | July 31 | Cash | CB 23 | 1,298.72 |

If we took the balance on the accounts shown in this example as at 31 July 20X7 the list of balances would be as follows.

TRIAL BALANCE 31/7/X7

| | *Debit* £ | *Credit* £ |
|---|---|---|
| Cash (all receipts) | 3,082.00 | |
| Debtors | 200.00 | |
| VAT | | 488.80 |
| Sales - hardware | | 1,366.82 |
| Sales – electrical | | 1,426.38 |
| | 3,282.00 | 3,282.00 |

This must **include** the balances on control accounts, but **exclude** the balances on the personal accounts in the sales ledger, which are memorandum accounts.

### Activity 6.3

Your supervisor informs you that the following information for the year ended 31 May 20X7 comes from the accounting records of Supernova Ltd.

| | £ |
|---|---|
| Sales ledger control account as at 1 June 20X6 | |
| Debit balance | 12,404.86 |
| Credit balance | 322.94 |
| Credit sales | 96,464.41 |
| Goods returned from trade debtors | 1,142.92 |
| Payments received from trade debtors | 94,648.71* |
| Discounts allowed to trade debtors | 3,311.47** |

* This figures includes cheques totalling £192.00 which were dishonoured before 31 May 20X7, the debts in respect of which remained outstanding at 31 May 20X7. The only sales ledger account with a credit balance at 31 May 20X7 was that of ENR Ltd with a balance of £337.75.

** The discounts are all settlement discounts, taken against invoice values.

You are told that, after the preparation of the sales ledger control account for the year ended 31 May 20X7 from the information given above, the following accounting errors were discovered.

(i) In July 20X7, a debt due of £77.00 from PAL Ltd had been written off as bad. Whilst the correct entries have been made in PAL Ltd's personal account, no reference to the debt being written off has been made in the sales ledger control account.

(ii) Cash sales of £3,440.00 in November 20X6 have been included in the payments received from trade debtors of £94,648.71.

(iii) The sales day book for January 20X7 had been undercast by £427.80.

(iv) Credit sales £96,464.41 includes goods costing £3,711.86 returned to suppliers by Ultramarine Ltd.

(v) No entries have been made in the personal accounts for goods returned from trade debtors of £1,142.92.

(vi) The debit side of FTR Ltd's personal account has been overcast by £71.66.

**Tasks**

(a) Prepare the sales ledger control account for the year ended 31 May 20X7 as it would have been *before* the various accounting errors outlined above were discovered.

(b) Prepare a computation of the amount arising from the sales ledger to be shown as trade debtors as at 31 May 20X7.

*Helping hand.* Think carefully whether all the errors listed affect the control account.

## 5 PURPOSE OF THE DEBTORS CONTROL ACCOUNT

5.1 There are a number of reasons for having a debtors control account, mainly to do with the usefulness of **reconciling the control account to the list of memorandum sales ledger balances.**

| Purpose | Details |
|---|---|
| **To check the accuracy of entries** made in the personal accounts | Comparing the balance on the debtors control account with the total of individual balances on the sales ledger personal accounts means we can identify the fact that errors have been made. |
| To **trace errors** | By using the debtors control account, a comparison with the individual balances in the sales ledger can be made for **every week** or **day** of the month, and the error found much more quickly than if a control account like this did not exist. |
| To provide an **internal check** | The person posting entries to the debtors control account will act as a check on a different person whose job it is to post entries to the sales ledger accounts. |
| To provide a **debtors balance quickly** | This is useful when producing a trial balance. |

## 6 DEBTORS CONTROL ACCOUNT RECONCILIATION

6.1 The debtors control account should be **balanced regularly** (at least monthly), and the balance on the account **agreed to the sum of the individual debtors' balances** extracted from the sales ledger.

6.2 In practice, more often than not the balance on the control account does not agree with the sum of balances extracted, for one or more of the following reasons.

| Reason for disagreement | How to correct |
|---|---|
| **Miscast of the total in the book of prime entry** (adding up incorrectly). | The main ledger debit and credit postings will balance, but the debtors control account balance will not agree with the sum of individual balances extracted from the (memorandum) sales ledger. A journal entry must then be made in the main ledger to correct the debtors control account and the corresponding sales account. |
| A **transposition error** in **posting** an individual's transaction from the book of prime entry to the memorandum ledger. | For example the sale to C Collins of £250 might be posted to his account as £520. The **sum of balances** extracted from the memorandum ledger **must be corrected**. No accounting entry would be required to do this, except to alter the figure in C Collins' account. |
| **Omission of a transaction from the debtors control account or the memorandum account, but not both.** | A single entry will correct an omission from the memorandum account in the sales ledger. Where a transaction is missing from the debtors control account, then the double entry will have to be checked and corrected. |
| The **sum of balances** extracted from the sales ledger may be **incorrectly extracted** or **miscast**. | Correct the total of the balances. |

6.3 Reconciling the debtors control account balance with the sum of the balances extracted from the (memorandum) sales ledger is an important procedure. It should be performed **regularly** so that any errors are revealed and appropriate action can be taken. The reconciliation should be done in five steps.

***Step 1*** Balance the accounts in the memorandum ledger, and review for errors.

***Step 2*** Correct the total of the balances extracted from the memorandum ledger.

| | £ | £ |
|---|---|---|
| Sales ledger total | | |
| Original total extracted | | 15,320 |
| Add difference arising from transposition error (£95 written as £59) | | 36 |
| | | 15,356 |
| Less | | |
| Credit balance of £60 extracted as a debit balance (£60 × 2) | 120 | |
| Overcast of list of balances | 90 | |
| | | (210) |
| | | 15,146 |

***Step 3*** Balance the debtors control account, and review for errors.

***Step 4*** Adjust or post the debtors control account **with correcting entries.**

***Step 5*** Prepare a statement showing how the corrected sales ledger agrees to the corrected debtors control account.

DEBTORS CONTROL ACCOUNT

| | £ | | £ |
|---|---|---|---|
| Balance before adjustments | 15,091 | Returns inwards: individual posting omitted from control a/c | 45 |
| | | Balance c/d | 15,146 |
| Undercast of total invoices issued in sales day book | 100 | (now in agreement with the corrected total of individual balances above) | |
| | 15,191 | | 15,191 |
| Balance b/d | 15,146 | | |

Once the five steps are completed, the total sales ledger balances should equal the debtors control account balance.

6.4 The debtors control account reconciliation will be carried out by the **sales ledger clerk** and reviewed and approved by a **senior member of staff.**

## Activity 6.4

(a) You are an employee of Ultrabrite Ltd and have been asked to help prepare the end of year accounts for the period ended 30 November 20X7 by agreeing the figure for total debtors.

The following figures, relating to the financial year, have been obtained from the books of original entry.

| | £ |
|---|---|
| Purchases for the year | 361,947 |
| Sales | 472,185 |
| Returns inwards | 41,226 |
| Returns outwards | 16,979 |
| Bad debts written off | 1,914 |
| Discounts allowed | 2,672 |
| Discounts received | 1,864 |
| Cheques paid to creditors | 342,791 |
| Cheques received from debtors | 429,811 |
| Customer cheques dishonoured | 626 |

You discover that at the close of business on 30 November 20X6 the total of the debtors amounted to £50,241.

*Task*

Prepare Ultrabrite Ltd's sales ledger control account for the year ended 30 November 20X7.

(b) To give you some assistance, your rather inexperienced colleague, Peter Johnson, has attempted to extract and total the individual balances in the sales ledger. He provides you with the following listing which he has prepared.

| | £ |
|---|---|
| Bury plc | 7,500 |
| P Fox & Son (Swindon) Ltd | 2,000 |
| Frank Wendlebury & Co Ltd | 4,297 |
| D Richardson & Co Ltd | 6,847 |
| Ultra Ltd | 783 |
| Lawrenson Ltd | 3,765 |
| Walkers plc | 4,091 |
| P Fox & Son (Swindon) Ltd | 2,000 |
| Whitchurch Ltd | 8,112 |
| Ron Bradbury & Co Ltd | 5,910 |
| Anderson Ltd | 1,442 |
| | 46,347 |

Subsequent to the drawing up of the list, the following errors have so far been found.

(i) A sales invoice for £267 sent to Whitchurch Ltd had been correctly entered in the day book but had not then been posted to the account for Whitchurch Ltd in the sales ledger.

(ii) One of the errors made by Peter Johnson (you suspect that his list may contain others) was to omit the £2,435 balance of Rectofon Ltd from the list.

(iii) A credit note for £95 sent to Bury plc had been correctly entered in the day book but was entered in the account in the sales ledger as £75.

**Task**

Prepare a statement reconciling the £46,347 total provided by Peter Johnson with the balance of your own sales ledger control account.

## Integrated accounting systems

6.5 In a computerised accounting system, different parts of the system (for example, the main ledger, the sales ledger and the purchase ledger) may be 'integrated'.

> **KEY TERM**
>
> **Intregated accounting systems.** The posting of transactions to the different ledgers is carried out by the **computer software,** without the need for different steps as in the case of a manual system.

6.6 In a **non-integrated system**, the different operations involved are not combined.

(a) A posting must be made to the sales ledger **and** a posting must also be made to the debtors control account in the main ledger.

(b) This gives rise to the need for day books, which list and produce summary totals of transactions for posting in summarised form to the debtors control account.

(c) A non-integrated system of ledgers may be either computer-based or not computer-based.

6.7 In an **integrated system**, postings to the sales ledger are carried out automatically in the same way as the corresponding posting to the debtors control account in the main ledger.

(a) Differences between the debtors control account and the total of the individual sales ledger accounts might still arise, however. This is because in any accounting system, adjustments may be made to accounts by the different method of using **the journal**.

(b) There will still then be a need to perform a debtors control account reconciliation.

## Key learning points

- A **control account** is an account which **keeps a total record for a collective item** (for example debtors) which in reality consists of many individual items (for example individual debtors). It is an impersonal account maintained in the nominal ledger.
- The **sales ledger control account** (or '**debtors control account**') is a **record of the total of the balances owed by customers**. Postings are made from the sales and sales returns day books, the cash book and the journal, in order to maintain this record.
- The **debtors control account serves a number of purposes.**
  - It provides a check on the accuracy of entries made in the personal sales ledger accounts, and helps with the tracing of any errors which may have occurred.
  - It also provides an internal check on employees' work.
  - It gives a convenient total debtors balance when the time comes to produce a trial balance or a balance sheet.
- The **balance on the debtors control account** should be **reconciled regularly with the sum of the memorandum sales ledger account balances** so that any necessary action can be taken.

## Quick quiz

1 What is a control account?

2 What does the balance on the debtors control account represent?

3 A dishonoured cheque is a credit entry in the debtors control account. True or false?

4 How might a credit balance arise in the debtors control account?

5 What is a trial balance?

6 Why might the balance on the debtors control account not agree with the total of the individual debtors' balances?

## Answers to quick quiz

1 An account in which a record is kept of the total value of a number of similar but individual items.

2 The total amount due to the business from its debtors.

3 False. Cash received is a credit entry, therefore a dishonoured cheque must be a debit.

4 A customer may return goods or overpay his balance.

5 A list of all the balances in the main ledger at any one time.

6 (i) There may be a transposition error in posting an individual's transaction from the book of prime entry to the memorandum ledger.

(ii) The day book could be miscast.

(iii) A transaction may be omitted from the control account or the memorandum account.

(iv) The total may be incorrectly extracted.

# 7 Creditors control account

## This chapter contains



## Learning objectives

On completion of this chapter you will be able to:

- Total and reconcile the creditors control account in the main ledger with the total of creditors' balances in the purchase ledger
- Identify and deal with discrepancies arising from the reconciliation of the creditors control account

### Performance criteria

3.2 Relevant accounts are totalled

3.2 Control accounts are reconciled with the totals of the balances in the subsidiary ledger, where appropriate

3.2 Authorised adjustments are correctly processed and documented

3.2 Discrepancies arising from the reconciliation of control accounts are either resolved or referred to the appropriate person

### Range statement

3.2.1 Ledgers: main ledger; sub-ledger; integrated ledger

3.2.2 Control accounts: creditors

3.2.3 Adjustments: to correct errors

### Knowledge and understanding

- Identification of different types of error
- Relationship between the accounting system and the ledger
- Reconciling control accounts with memorandum accounts

## 1 INTRODUCTION

1.1 Now you know how the debtors control account works, you should find it fairly easy to master the creditors control account.

### ASSESSMENT ALERT

The control accounts you need to know about are

**Debtors** - covered in Chapter 6
**Creditors** - covered here
**Stock** - covered in Chapter 5
**Cash** - covered in Chapter 5 and Unit 1
**Wages and salaries** - covered in Chapter 5 and Unit 2

## 2 PURPOSE OF THE CREDITORS CONTROL ACCOUNT

2.1 The two control accounts which you will encounter most frequently in accounting systems are the control accounts for total debtors and for total creditors.

(a) The balance on the debtors control account or sales ledger control account (SLCA) will be the **total amount due to the business at that time from its debtors.**

(b) The balance on the creditors control account or purchase ledger control account (PLCA) at any time will be the **total amount owed by the business at that time to its creditors.**

2.2 The creditors control account or PLCA records all of the transactions involving the creditors of the business.

2.3 The creditors control account, like the debtors control account, provides:

- A check on the **accuracy of entries** in the individual personal accounts
- Help in **locating errors**
- A form of **internal check**
- A total trade creditors' balance for when a **trial balance** or balance sheet needs to be prepared

## How the control account works

2.4 It works very much like the sales ledger control account.

***Step 1*** The **purchase day book** records the individual purchase invoices and credit notes which a business receives (unless there is also a purchase returns day book).

***Step 2*** Each invoice is recorded individually in the appropriate personal account in the **purchase ledger** for the supplier from whom the invoice or credit note has been received.

***Step 3*** The personal accounts for creditors are, in many accounting systems, **memorandum accounts** and do not as such form a part of the double entry system of accounting.

***Step 4*** The total purchase invoice and credit note transactions shown in the day books can be posted to the main ledger using **double entry.**

---

### Activity 7.1

Which one of the following statements describes the relationship between the **purchase ledger control account and the purchase ledger?**

A The **purchase ledger control account** is where the corresponding debit side of credit entries to the **purchase ledger** are posted.

B The **purchase ledger control account** is where invoices from customers for whom you have not set up an account in the **purchase ledger** are posted.

C The **purchase ledger** is a memorandum list of invoices and related transactions analysed by customer. The **purchase ledger control account** is the total of creditor balances, and is in the balance sheet.

D The **purchase ledger** forms part of the double entry. The **purchase ledger control account** is a memorandum control total used for internal checking purposes.

---

## 3 POSTING TO THE CREDITORS CONTROL ACCOUNT

3.1 Typical entries in the creditors control account are shown in the example below. The references PDB and PRDB are to the purchase day book and purchase returns day book respectively.

CREDITORS CONTROL ACCOUNT

| | Folio | £ | | Folio | £ |
|---|---|---|---|---|---|
| Opening debit balances | b/d | 70 | Opening credit balances | b/d | 8,300 |
| Cash paid | CB | 29,840 | Purchases and other expenses | PDB | 31,000 |
| Discounts received | CB | 30 | Cash received clearing debit balances | CB | 20 |
| Returns outwards | PRDB | 60 | Closing debit balances | c/d | 80 |
| Closing credit balances | c/d | 9,400 | | | |
| | | 39,400 | | | 39,400 |
| Debit balances | b/d | 80 | Credit balances | b/d | 9,400 |

3.2 Let's consider these entries in more detail.

| **Debit entries** | **Double entry** |
|---|---|
| Opening debit balances | This is unusual, perhaps an overpayment to a creditor, or a payment made before a supplier has sent an invoice. |
| Cash paid | **Credit** cash, **debit** total creditors. |
| Discounts received | The debit is the difference between the full amount invoiced by suppliers and the discounted amount which we paid. **Debit** total creditors **credit** discounts received. |
| Returns outwards | These are returns of goods to suppliers recorded as credit notes received. **Debit** total creditors, **credit** purchases. |
| Closing credit balances | Represent the **total** of the creditors carried down. |

| **Credit entries** | **Double entry** |
|---|---|
| Opening credit balances | Represent total creditors brought down (disregarding any debit balances). |
| Purchases and other expenses | The amounts invoiced by suppliers. **Debit** purchases, **credit** total creditors. |
| Cash received clearing debit balances | An unusual item. **Debit** cash, **credit** total creditors. |
| Closing debit balances | Carried down separately from credit balances. |

## 3.3 EXAMPLE: CONTROL ACCOUNTS

The following example involves both debtors and creditors control accounts.

On examining the books of Steps Ltd, you discover that on 1 October 20X1 the sales ledger balances were £8,024 debit and £57 credit, and the purchase ledger balances on the same date were £6,235 credit and £105 debit.

For the year ended 30 September 20X2 the following details are available.

| | £ |
|---|---|
| Sales | 63,728 |
| Purchases | 39,974 |
| Cash received from debtors | 55,212 |
| Cash paid to creditors | 37,307 |
| Discount received | 1,475 |
| Discount allowed | 2,328 |
| Returns inwards | 1,002 |
| Returns outwards | 535 |
| Bad debts written off | 326 |
| Cash received in respect of debit balances in purchase ledger | 105 |
| Amount due from customer as shown by sales ledger, offset against amount due to the same firm as shown by purchase ledger (settlement by contra) | 434 |

On 30 September 20X2 there were no credit balances in the sales ledger except those outstanding on 1 October 20X1, and no debit balances in the purchase ledger.

We need to write up the following accounts recording the above transactions and bringing down balances as on 30 September 20X2.

(a) Debtors control account
(b) Creditors control account

## 3.4 SOLUTION

DEBTORS CONTROL ACCOUNT

| | | | | | |
|---|---|---|---|---|---|
| 20X1 | | £ | 20X1 | | £ |
| Oct 1 | Balances b/d | 8,024 | Oct 1 | Balances b/d | 57 |
| 20X2 | | | 20X2 | | |
| Sept 30 | Sales | 63,728 | Sept 30 | Cash received from debtors | 55,212 |
| | Balances c/d | 57 | | Discount allowed | 2,328 |
| | | | | Returns inwards | 1,002 |
| | | | | Bad debts written off | 326 |
| | | | | Transfer control creditors account | 434 |
| | | | | Balances c/d | 12,450 |
| | | 71,809 | | | 71,809 |

CREDITORS CONTROL ACCOUNT

| | | | | | |
|---|---|---|---|---|---|
| 20X1 | | £ | 20X1 | | £ |
| Oct 1 | Balances b/d | 105 | Oct 1 | Balances b/d | 6,235 |
| 20X2 | | | 20X2 | | |
| Sept 30 | Cash paid to creditors | 37,307 | Sept 30 | Purchases | 39,974 |
| | Discount received | 1,475 | | Cash | 105 |
| | Returns outwards | 535 | | | |
| | Transfer debtors control account | 434 | | | |
| | Balances c/d | 6,458 | | | |
| | | 46,314 | | | 46,314 |

# 4 CREDITORS CONTROL ACCOUNT RECONCILIATION

4.1 There are good reasons for performing this reconciliation.

(a) The account should be **balanced regularly.**

(b) The balance on the account should be agreed with the sum of the individual creditors' balances extracted from the purchase ledger.

As with the debtors control account, this routine will be carried out on a monthly basis in many businesses.

4.2 **Items in the reconciliation** are likely to arise from similar occurrences to those already identified in the case of the debtors control account discussed in Chapter 6.

| Error | Affects |
|---|---|
| • Miscast of purchase day book or cash book | Creditors control account |
| • Transposition error in entry from day book to purchase ledger | Purchase ledger balances |
| • Missing entries in *either* purchase ledger *or* control account | *Either* purchase ledger *or* control account |
| • Miscast of total purchase ledger balances | Purchase ledger balances |
| • Miscast of creditors control account | Creditors control account |

4.3 The reconciliation of the creditors control account should be carried out in five steps.

***Step 1*** Balance the account in the memorandum ledger, and review for errors.

***Step 2*** Correct the total of the balances extracted from the memorandum purchase ledger.

***Step 3*** Balance the creditors control account, and review for errors.

***Step 4*** Adjust or post the necessary correcting entries to the account.

***Step 5*** Prepare a statement showing how the corrected purchase ledger agrees to the corrected creditors control account.

4.4 In the example below, it is necessary to write up the account for the year and then to prepare the **control account reconciliation statement.**

## Activity 7.2

A computerised accounting system contains three modules:

(a) General ledger
(b) Purchase ledger
(c) Sales ledger

The system is an **integrated** one. This means that postings to the **main ledger** are made **automatically** from the sales and purchase ledgers.

In this situation, indicate whether the following statement is TRUE or FALSE.

| | | *Tick* |
|---|---|---|
| The creditors control account total will *always* agree with the sum of the balances on the individual creditor accounts in the purchase ledger, and no disagreement is ever possible | True | ☐ |
| | False | ☐ |

## Activity 7.3

(a) Which, if any, of the following could you see in a reconciliation of the creditors control account with the purchase ledger list of balances?

   (i) Mispostings of cash payments to suppliers
   (ii) Casting errors
   (iii) Transposition errors

(b) Which of the following would you not expect to see reflected in a *creditors control account*?

   (i) Dividend payments
   (ii) Invoices received, in summary
   (iii) Drawings
   (iv) Cheque payments
   (v) Contras
   (vi) Returns to suppliers
   (vii) Debit notes to suppliers
   (viii) Discounts received

(c) You would never see a debit balance on a purchase ledger account.

| | *Tick* |
|---|---|
| True | ☐ |
| False | ☐ |

## 4.5 EXAMPLE: CONTROL ACCOUNT RECONCILIATION

Minster plc at present makes use of a manual system of accounting consisting of a main ledger, a sales ledger and a purchase ledger together with books of prime entry. The various accounts within the ledgers are drawn up on ledger cards which are updated by hand from the books of prime entry when relevant transactions take place. The decision has now been taken to use a control account in the main ledger to help keep a check on the purchase ledger and the following figures relating to the financial year ended 31 October 20X1 have been extracted from the books of prime entry.

| | £ |
|---|---|
| Credit purchases | 132,485 |
| Cash purchases | 18,917 |
| Credit notes received from credit suppliers | 2,361 |
| Discounts received from credit suppliers | 4,153 |
| Cheques paid to credit suppliers | 124,426 |
| Balances in the sales ledger set off against balances in the purchase ledger | 542 |

On 1 November 20X0 the total of the creditors was £28,603.

The purchase ledger accounts have been totalled at £28,185 as at 31 October 20X1.

Subsequent to the totalling procedure, the following matters are discovered.

(a) Whilst the totalling was taking place the chief accountant was reviewing the account of Peterbury Ltd, a supplier, and the ledger card was on his desk. The balance of the account at 31 October was £1,836.

(b) A credit note for £387 issued by John Danbury Ltd, a credit supplier, was correctly entered in the day book but had not then been posted to John Danbury Ltd's account in the ledger.

(c) An invoice for £1,204 issued by Hartley Ltd, a credit supplier, was correctly entered in the day book and was then entered in Hardy Ltd's account in the purchase ledger.

(d) An invoice for £898 relating to a credit purchase from Intergram plc, although correctly entered in the day book, was posted to the supplier's account in the ledger as £889.

(e) A discount for £37 allowed to Minster plc by the credit supplier K Barden Ltd, had been correctly entered in the cash book but was then omitted from the company's account in the ledger.

*Tasks*

(a) Prepare Minster plc's creditors control account for the year ended 31 October 20X1.

(b) Prepare a statement reconciling the original total of the purchase ledger accounts with the balance of your creditors control account.

## 4.6 SOLUTION

### Steps 1, 2 and 5

| | £ | £ |
|---|---|---|
| Balance as per listing of creditors' accounts | | 28,185 |
| Add | | |
| Peterbury Ltd ledger card omitted | 1,836 | |
| Posting error (Intergram plc) | 9 | |
| | | 1,845 |
| | | 30,030 |
| Less | | |
| Credit note not posted | 387 | |
| Discount received (K Barden Ltd) | 37 | |
| | | 424 |
| Balance as per creditors control account | | 29,606 |

*Note*. Item (c), the invoice from Hartley Ltd, has been treated correctly and therefore no adjustment is required.

### Steps 3 and 4

CREDITORS CONTROL ACCOUNT

| | £ | | £ |
|---|---|---|---|
| Credit notes received | 2,361 | Balance b/d | 28,603 |
| Discounts received | 4,153 | Purchases | 132,485 |
| Bank | 124,426 | | |
| Contra sales ledger | 542 | | |
| Balance c/d | 29,606 | | |
| | 161,088 | | 161,088 |

## Integrated accounting systems

4.7 When we looked at the debtors control account in Chapter 6 we noted that, in a computerised system, different parts of the accounting system may be '**integrated**' together. Similar points apply to the purchase ledger as well.

### Activity 7.4

You are employed by Wallace & Grommet, a partnership. You have ascertained that as at 31 July 20X7 the creditors control account balance of £57,997.34 does not agree with the total of the balances extracted from the purchase ledger of £54,842.40.

On investigation, some errors come to light.

(i) An account with a balance of £8,300.00 had been omitted from the purchase ledger balances.

(ii) Purchases of £7,449.60 for June had not been credited to the creditors control account.

(iii) RNH Ltd's account in the purchase ledger had been undercast by £620.40.

(iv) A van bought on credit for £6,400.00 had been credited to the creditors control account.

(v) Returns outwards of £1,424.50 had been omitted from the creditors control account.

(vi) A cheque for £5,000.00 payable to SPL Ltd had not been debited to its account in the purchase ledger.

(vii) Discounts received of £740.36 had been entered twice in the creditors control account.

(viii) A contra arrangement of £400.00 with a trade debtor had not been set off in the purchase ledger.

*Helping hand.* With item (vi), think carefully whether you are adding or deducting.

**Task**

Set out the necessary adjustments to:

(a) The schedule of balances as extracted from the purchase ledger
(b) The balance in the creditors control account

## And finally ...

4.8 Look back to the diagram in Section 2 of Chapter 2. Now you know about control accounts, it will all fall into place!

## Key learning points

- The **creditors control account (CCA) (or purchase ledger control account)** records the true total of the balances owed to credit suppliers. This record is prepared from postings from the purchase and purchase returns day books, the cash book and the journal.
- The CCA **acts as a check on the accuracy of individual suppliers' accounts** in the purchase ledger, as well as acting as a **form of internal check**. If a trial balance or balance sheet is needed, a total trade creditors' balance can be extracted from the account.
- The **balance on the CCA should be reconciled regularly with the sum of the memorandum purchase ledger account balances.**

## Quick quiz

1 What does the balance on the purchase ledger control account (creditors control account) represent?

2 Name two uses of a purchase ledger control account.

3 Discounts received from suppliers are credited to the creditors control account. True or false?

4 What is the double entry for cash received to clear a debit balance on the creditors control account?

5 The purchase day book is miscast. Would this affect the creditors control account or the purchase ledger?

6 An invoice has been incorrectly entered in the purchase day book. Would this give rise to a difference between the creditors control account and the total of purchase ledger balances?

## Answers to quick quiz

1 The total amount owed by the business to its creditors.

2 (i) Checks accuracy of entries in the personal accounts.
(ii) Provides a total creditors figure for the list of balances.

3 False. They are debited.

4 DEBIT Cash
CREDIT Creditors control account

5 The creditors control account.

6 No. Both would be incorrect.

# *Part C*

## *Filing*

# 8 Filing

## This chapter contains



## Learning objectives

On completion of this chapter you will be able to:

- Understand the organisation's procedures for filing informatiion

## Knowledge and understanding

- Relevant understanding of the organisation's business transactions
- Organisational procedures for filing source information

## 1 INTRODUCTION

1.1 So far we have talked a lot about processing documents and the accounting system. In this chapter we will look at ways of storing the information which we are going to use.

## 2 INFORMATION STORAGE

2.1 We are now going to look at the characteristics of a **filing system,** and at how files are organised and stored. This chapter should help you to deal with files in practice:

- Getting hold of them
- Finding documents within them
- Putting new documents into them

### The features of an information storage system

2.2 Information for business users takes many forms. Whatever form documents and recorded information take, if they are to be of any use, they must be maintained so that:

(a) **Authorised people** (and only authorised people) can get to the information they require quickly and easily

(b) Information can be **added to, updated and outdated** as necessary

(c) Information is **safe from fire, loss or handling damage** for as long as it is required (but not necessarily for ever)

(d) Accessibility, flexibility and security are achieved as **cheaply** as possible

### Files

**KEY TERM**

A **file** is a collection of data records with similar characteristics.

2.3 Here are some examples of files.

(a) A sales ledger

(b) A purchase ledger

(c) A cash book

(d) Stock records

(e) The nominal ledger

(f) A price list

(g) A collection of letters, memos and other papers all relating to the same matter, usually kept within a single folder

We will be talking mainly about **paper files** or **manual files** in this chapter; you should bear in mind, however, that **electronic files** can be created and used in a computer system as well.

2.4 Files of data may be **temporary, permanent, active,** and **non-active.**

(a) **Master files** and **reference files** are usually **permanent**, which means that they are never thrown away or scrapped. They will be **updated** from time to time, and so the information on the file might change, but the file itself will continue to exist.

(b) A **temporary file** is one that is eventually scrapped. Many **transaction files** are held for a very short time, until the transaction records have been processed, but are then thrown away. Other transaction files are permanent (for example a cash book) or are held for a considerable length of time before being scrapped.

(c) An **active file** is one that is frequently used, for example, sales invoice files relating to the current financial year, or correspondence files relating to current customers and suppliers.

(d) A **non-active file** is one that is no longer used on a day-to-day basis. For example, files that contain information relating to customers and suppliers who are no longer current, and purchase invoices relating to previous financial periods.

2.5 Apart from these basic records - grouped items of information - about, say, personnel, sales or stock, there are huge amounts of information passing through organisations needing to be kept track of. Consider the following examples.

- Letters, memos, telegrams, telexes, emails
- Notes of phone calls and meetings
- Reports
- Advertising material and press cuttings
- Mailing lists
- Important/routine addresses and phone numbers
- Machinery documents such as guarantees or service logs
- Legal documents such as contracts, property deeds or insurance policies

## Characteristics of a filing system

2.6 Can you suggest what characteristics a 'good' file should possess?

Possibly some or all of these.

(a) It should **contain all the information** you might want to look up.

(b) It should allow you to **find particular information easily**.

(c) It needs to be of a **convenient size**.

(d) It needs to have **room for expansion**.

(e) The file should be **stored close to you** and/or should be easy to get to when it is needed.

(f) The method used for storage should be **strong and secure** so that the file will not get damaged and information will not get lost.

2.7 A **filing system** for an entire organisation is not really much different. It should:

(a) **Contain all the information** that users might want

(b) Be classified and indexed in such as way as to make it **easy to find information** quickly

(c) Be **suited to the people who will use it**

(d) Be **reliable and secure**

(e) Be **flexible** enough to allow for expansion

(f) Be **cost-effective** to install and maintain. There is no point spending more to hold information on file than the information is actually worth

(g) Allow users to **retrieve information quickly**

---

### Activity 8.1

Your organisation has just received the following letter. List the details that are likely to be used when deciding where it should be filed. What other department would you send a copy of the letter to?

**SANDIMANS LTD**

72 High Street, Epsom
Surrey EP12 4AB

Your reference: Z/0335/MJD
Our reference: BRC/1249/871

Mr G Latchmore
Purchasing Department
Lightfoot & Co
7 West Broughton St
LONDON W12 9LM

4 May 20X6

Dear Mr Latchmore

***Stationery supplies***

I refer to your letter of 11 April 20X6.

I am afraid that we are still unable to trace receipt of your payment of £473.20 in settlement of our invoice number 147829. I should be grateful if you would look into this and issue a fresh cheque if necessary.

Your sincerely

*Mandy Sands*

Mandy Sands

---

2.8 So, with all of this information floating around, how are we going to locate a particular item of information? We need to make sure that our information is held in an organised fashion, and that we have procedures in place so we can find what we are looking for quickly and easily.

## 3 CLASSIFYING, INDEXING AND CROSS-REFERENCING INFORMATION

### Classifying information

3.1 Information has to be filed in such a way that its **users know where it is and how to retrieve it** later when it is needed. This means having different files for different types of information, and then **holding each file in a particular order.** Information in an individual file might be divided into categories and then held in a particular order within each category.

> **KEY TERM**
>
> **Classification** is the process of grouping related items of information together into categories that reflect the relationship between them.

3.2 There are various ways in which information can be grouped together, or **classified**.

(a) By **name** (for example correspondence relating to a particular person or company).

(b) By **geography** (for example all documents relating to a particular country, area or city).

(c) By **subject matter** (for example all documents relating to a particular contract, transaction or type of problem).

(d) By **date** (for example all invoices for a certain month or year).

(e) By **department** (for example profits or costs for each department or employees of each department).

3.3 Once broad classifications are established, the material can be **put into a sequence** which will make individual items easier to retrieve. Again there are various systems for arranging files.

(a) **Alphabetical order** - for example customers listed in name order.

(b) **Numerical order** - for example invoices listed in numerical order of invoice numbers.

(c) **Alpha-numerical** (A1, A2, A3, B1, B2 and so on).

(d) **Chronological order** - for example letters within a subject file listed by the date they were written.

3.4 These ways of subdividing and arranging data in a logical way within suitable categories make it possible to store, find and also **index** or **cross-reference** information efficiently.

Let us have a look at some of these systems for arranging information.

### Alphabetical classification

3.5 The most common means of classification is **alphabetical.** In an alphabetical name system items are filed according to the first and then each following letter of a person's or company's name (for example in the phone book). This sounds simple enough, and indeed it is most of the time, but there are some rules which must be followed .

3.6 **Surnames**. The system works by surname. The hyphen is ignored in double-barrelled names. When surnames are the same, initials or first names are taken into account. All of this is illustrated below.

Dawson
Ullyott
Vivian
Watkins
Williams
Williams
Williamson
Winters, Douglas
Winters, George

3.7 **Initials.** Names made up of initials may come before whole-word names.

PBAB Parties Ltd
Party Time Ltd

3.8 **Prefixes** are included as part of the surname.

De Beauvoir
Le Bon
McVitee
Von Richthofen

3.9 Mc, Mac etc are all treated as if they were Mac, so:

McGraw
MacLaverty

and St is usually treated as Saint, so:

St Angela's Convent
Saint George's Chapel.

3.10 **Titles and common words.** Words such as 'Mr', 'Mrs', 'Sir', 'The', 'A' are ignored for filing purposes (or most names would be under M or T!) while departments, ministries, offices, local authorities and so on are filed under the key part of their name:

Stanwick, B (Mrs)
Stock Exchange (The)
Trend, N U (Prof)
Finance, Ministry of

Bromley, London Borough of
Fair Trading, Department of
Foreign Office

3.11 **Businesses** with names like 'Phillip Smith Ltd', 'Frank Tilsley & Son, are sometimes listed under the first letter of the surname (as usual) but perhaps more often under the first letter of the whole name (P and F in the examples given).

3.12 **Numbers** which appear as names may also count as if they were spelled out as words:

84 Charing Cross Road (under 'E' for Eighty)
2001: A Space Odyssey (under 'T' for Two)
3i plc (under 'T' for Three).

3.13 You will find things arranged differently in some cases. Rules do vary from system to system. **Get to know the ones you have to work with in your organisation.**

3.14 The **alphabetical name system** is used, for example, in files of clients or customers, students, employees or members and also for index cards and cross-referencing (which we will come to a bit later). It is a simple to use and easily expandable system: there is a 'right' place for files, so they can simply be taken out or slotted in as necessary.

## Numerical classification

3.15 **Numerical sequence** is natural where standard documents are concerned. Invoices, for example, are numbered: if one needs to be checked, the number need only be established (quoted by the enquirer, or looked up in the customer account perhaps) and can be easily found. This is known as a **numerical-sequential** system.

3.16 Numerical classification is very **flexible**. Unlike the alphabetical method, you do not have to decide how much filing space to allocate to each letter, wasting space if you are too generous and having to shuffle the whole system along if you are too 'mean'. With numerical order, you simply give a new file the next number and position in the system.

3.17 On the other hand, numbers may not be very meaningful in isolation. A strict **alphabetical index** also has to be kept, and also a **numerical file list** or **accession register**, in order to establish the file number to look for. It also means that there is little room for subdivisions for easier identification and retrieval, although blocks of numbers can be allotted to different departments, say.

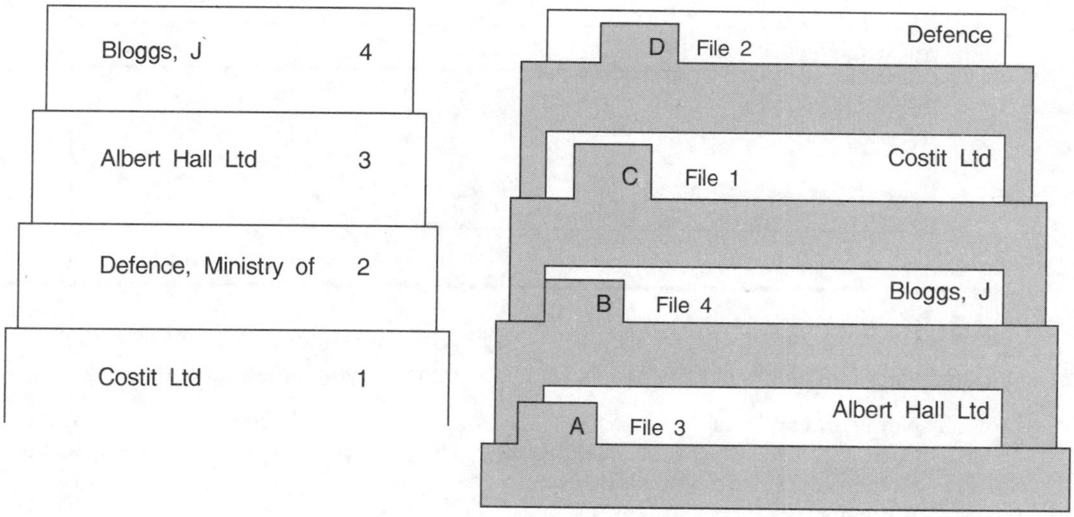


## Alpha-numeric classification

3.18 In an **alpha-numeric system** files are given a reference consisting of **letters** and **numbers**. For example a letter received from Mr Blotson about the purchase of a flat in Mayfair might be given the reference BLO/8745/99/1.

(a) The system uses the first three letters of the correspondent's name and a number to distinguish him from anybody else called Blotson and/or to indicate that the subject matter is domestic property. The number 99 indicates that this correspondence began in 1999.

(b) The 1 shows that it is the first file which has anything to do with this subject. If Mr Blotson's property deal fell through but he then found another flat the correspondence relating to this would be kept in the separate but related file BLO/8745/97/2.

3.19 A system like this is most useful where there is a very large volume of correspondence on different but related topics. The Civil Service, for example, uses a system along these lines.

## Other classifications

3.20 Using any of the above systems, bear in mind that you could group your files in any logical way. Common examples include:

(a) **Subject classification**, where all material relating to a particular subject (client, contract, project, product and so on) is kept together. (You just need to title your subjects thoughtfully, otherwise you end up with a lot of 'miscellaneous' items that do not fit your subject categories)

(b) **Geographical classification**, which is useful for sales, import/export and similar activities that may be organised by region or territory

Here is an example of geographical files, sub-classified by subject, in alphabetical order.

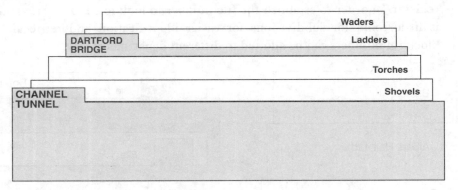


## Activity 8.2

Listed below are details of thirty people who have written to your organisation.

| | Name and address | Account | Date |
|---|---|---|---|
| 1 | Cottrell J, 5 Heathview Avenue, Bromley | - | 2.6.96 |
| 2 | Holden R, 27 Exning Road, Bexley | - | 13.7.95 |
| 3 | Williams J, 29 Gray Gardens, Dartford | 100276 | 5.4.97 |
| 4 | Bidwell D, 176 High Road, Dartford | - | 16.5.98 |
| 5 | Bexley J, 25 Romney Road, Orpington | 400452 | 17.5.95 |
| 6 | Maclean T, 1 Pitt Road, Orpington | 400721 | 7.12.98 |
| 7 | 54321 Discos, 107 Warren Road, Bexley | 300924 | 19.4.99 |
| 8 | Dr J Crown, 20 Wimfred Street, Woolwich | - | 1.1.96 |
| 9 | Locke D, 22 Davis Street, Crayford | - | 14.8.98 |
| 10 | Sainton E, 15 Filmwell Close, Bromley | 200516 | 3.5.99 |
| 11 | Argent-Smith M, 17a Waterson Road, Bexley | - | 7.8.99 |
| 12 | Britton T, 81 Ward Avenue, Crayford | - | 27.8.97 |
| 13 | McLaughlin D, 80 Brookhill Road, Orpington | 200435 | 4.3.97 |
| 14 | Williams J A, 148 Godstow Road, Woolwich | - | 6.6.99 |

| | | | |
|---|---|---|---|
| 15 | O'Grady E, 40 Holborne Road, Sidcup | 300989 | 4.4.94 |
| 16 | Saint Francis Pet Shop, 14 Glenesh Road, Dartford | - | 7.9.97 |
| 17 | Emly P, 8 Faraday Avenue, Orpington | - | 18.4.99 |
| 18 | Harry Holden Ltd, 5 Clare Way, Bexley | 100284 | 9.7.97 |
| 19 | BRJ Plumbing, 132 Lodge Lane, Crayford | 200223 | 25.11.98 |
| 20 | Gisling B, 18 Dickens Avenue, Woolwich | - | 6.3.99 |
| 21 | Argentson S, 20 Porson Court, Dartford | 400542 | 5.2.95 |
| 22 | Kelsey L C, 58 Cudham Lane, Bromley | - | 8.1.98 |
| 23 | ILD Services Ltd, 4 Cobden Road, Orpington | 200221 | 3.2.99 |
| 24 | Van Saintby A, 69 Brookhill Close, Bromley | 400693 | 5.2.99 |
| 25 | Williams, John, 10 Buff Close, Dartford | - | 2.12.98 |
| 26 | Page W, 11 Leewood Place, Crayford | 400442 | 9.7.96 |
| 27 | Harrison P, Robinwood Drive, Dartford | 101301 | 16.4.98 |
| 28 | Briton N, 3 Chalet Close, Bexley | - | 7.2.95 |
| 29 | Richmond A, 9 Denham Close, Crayford | - | 4.1.99 |
| 30 | St Olave's Church, Church Way, Bromley | 400371 | 21.2.98 |

**Tasks**

(a) Referring to the documents by number (1-30), in what order would they appear if they were filed in date order?

(b) Rearrange the names in alphabetical order, noting the reference number in brackets after the name.

(c) In what order would those correspondents with accounts appear if they were filed in account number order?

(d) Again referring to the documents by number, identify another sensible way of classifying them, and arrange them in this order.

*Helping hand.* Use coloured highlighter pens!

## 4 STORING DOCUMENTS SECURELY

### Environment

4.1 It is vital that material containing information is stored in an appropriate location and that its condition does not deteriorate.

4.2 Documents containing information may be classified and indexed so that they are easily accessible, but unless they can be kept in **good condition**, with **economy of storage space and cost**, they will not fulfil our requirements for an effective and efficient filing system.

### Keeping documents in good condition

4.3 Paper can very easily get screwed up, torn, stained, or otherwise damaged. This can result in its contents becoming difficult to read or even getting lost. For example tearing off the edge of a misaligned print-out could easily result in the final column of figures being thrown away.

4.4 Punching holes in a document so that it can be placed in some form of ring binder also needs to be carefully done so that vital numbers or words are not affected.

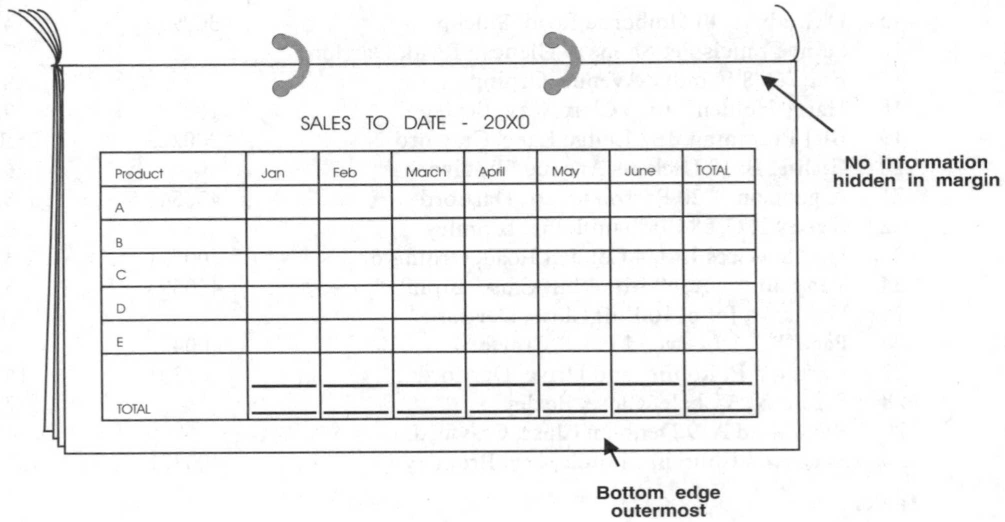


4.5 **If a file is too 'fat'** there is every likelihood that pages will get torn, fall out and get lost because of the difficulty of opening the file and keeping it open at the right page. If you need to be violent with a file it is not serving its purpose: you will be less inclined to consult the file and you run the risk of damaging its contents.

4.6 Obviously it is better not to let files get too fat in the first place, but if it is too late the best solution is to move some of the documents into a second volume. This may involve re-indexing the file or changing its title and altering any cross-references that have been made in the file itself or in other files.

4.7 **Liquid** and paper are not good friends: don't leave your coffee cup or your glass of water in places where you or somebody else is liable to knock them over.

## Location

4.8 Most documents containing information will have to be placed in **folders** or **binders** before they can be housed in filing cabinets or other forms of storage. These come in a suitable range of sizes (for small pieces of paper or large computer printouts) and materials.

4.9 **Plastic folders** or **paper envelope (manila) folders** are the most common and cheapest methods. For larger volumes of information, there are **lever arch files** and **box files**. If information is to be kept for a long time but not referred to very frequently, then box files are useful. If they are to be referred to and updated more often, ring binders or lever arch files would provide security (there would be no loose bits of paper flying about) but also accessibility.

## Storage equipment

4.10 The following items of equipment are commonly used to store information.

- In-trays
- Pigeon-holes
- Filing cabinets
- Safes

4.11 An **in-tray** is a tray which lies horizontally, and is used to capture incoming documentation. If you have your own in-tray at work, you will know that it is best to sort through new information on a regular basis! When sorting through an in-tray it is usual to group documents which are **ready for filing, awaiting action**, or **for distribution**.

4.12 The main purpose of an in-tray is therefore **temporary storage** of information.

4.13 A **pigeon-hole** is very similar to an in-tray, but incoming documents are held in a lateral rather than a horizontal position. In general, any incoming mail which is marked for your attention is placed in the first instance in your pigeon-hole. It is therefore also used as a **temporary store** for information.

4.14 Files containing information may be stored in an assortment of **filing cabinets**. The two main types of filing cabinet are **vertical suspension** and **lateral suspension**. The type of cabinet used will depend upon the space available in the office for such equipment, and the type of information to be stored.

## Safes

**KEY TERM**

A **safe** is a strong lockable cabinet which is used to store confidential or valuable information.

4.15 Most offices have some means of storing confidential or sensitive information. Safes normally have a **combination code** which must be entered correctly before they can be opened, and this code is normally known by one or two senior members of staff only.

**Activity 8.3**

Have a look around your office at work and look for examples of the different types of equipment that are used for storing and retrieving information.

## Microfilm and microfiche

4.16 **Microfilming** is a particularly convenient means of information storage for saving space. Documents are photographed into a very much reduced ('micro') form. Microfilms are readable, but not to the unassisted naked eye, and a magnifying reading device (with a viewing screen) is needed by users. **Microfilm** is itself a **continuous strip** with images in frames along its length (like a photographic negative).

Micro film

Micro fiche

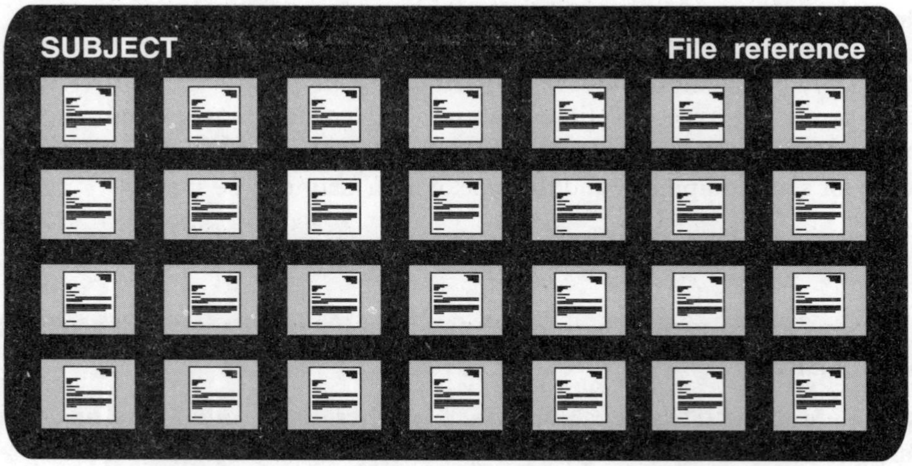


4.17 **Microfiche** is another method of storing information, but consists of **separate sheets of film**, rather than being a continuous strip like microfilm is. Microfiche is read by placing the fiche between two glass plates and moving a pointer (which is attached to the lens) across a grid. If you have never used a microfiche reader, see whether your local library has one, and have a practice.

4.18 Microfilm and microfiche need **special devices** in order to be read, updated or corrected. (If your organisation has 'computer aided retrieval' readers, see if you can get some coaching and practice on one.) However, they do offer very space-saving, durable and secure information storage.

## File security and confidentiality

4.19 If files are **confidential** or **secret**, they will be '**classified**', which means that access will be limited to authorised people. A list of classified files will be required and a policy must be drawn up stipulating **conditions of access** (for example who keeps the keys to the security cabinet, and whether files may be copied or taken out of the filing room) and specifying who has clearance to consult classified material.

4.20 Circumstances in which files may become classified include the following.

(a) Where they contain **information of a personal nature**, for example personnel files, or files about customers' credit status or (in a solicitor's office, say) his domestic circumstances.

(b) Where they contain **product or service information** which may be exploited by a competitor, like designs or marketing programmes.

(c) Where they contain **information concerning legal or financial deals**, the outcome of which could be affected by public knowledge of the details (for example when companies are considering merging or one is trying to take over another).

4.21 You can probably think of information which is '**sensitive**' in your organisation in that it could be misused to the organisation's disadvantage if it got into the wrong hands. If you are working on a 'classified' file, or if you have any reason to think documents in your possession may be of a sensitive nature, take care.

(a) Do not leave them lying around on your desk. **Put them away out of sight** when you are not using them, and lock them up if you have to leave your desk.

(b) Do not forget to **lock up secure cabinets** when you have finished with them, and return the keys to the authorised holder.

(c) **Do not send out copies** of potentially confidential material without checking with a superior that it is safe to do so.

(d) Do not leave confidential documents in the photocopier!

(e) **Respect the privacy of others,** just as you would expect them to respect yours.

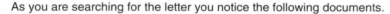

---

### Activity 8.4

Your manager is out of the office. He has phoned in and asked you to find a letter which is 'somewhere' on his desk and fax through a copy to him.

As you are searching for the letter you notice the following documents.

1 An electricity bill for £372.97 addressed to D Glover (your manager) at his home address.

2 A letter from a building society asking for a reference for one of your firm's clients.

3 A report entitled 'Potential Merger - Initial considerations'.

4 A mass of figures with your organisation's name at the head and the title 'Draft Budget'.

5 A staff appraisal report about you.

6 A thick sheaf of correspondence - the top sheet is signed 'Love, Nancy'.

7 A letter from P Glover asking for details about your organisation's services.

8 A *very* strongly worded letter of complaint from a Mrs Paribus.

9 A series of cuttings about your organisation from a trade journal.

10 A list of your organisation's directors with their addresses, telephone numbers and ages noted alongside.

**Tasks**

(a) Identify which, if any, of these documents you think should be filed away confidentially. Give reasons.

(b) Suppose that the letter that you had to fax was document 8 above. What would you do?

---

## Key learning points

- Information is generally held on **files. Filing** is an integral part of creating information.
- A **file** is a collection of data records with similar characteristics. Files of data may be **temporary, permanent, active** or **non-active.**

- Characteristics of a **'good' file** are as follows.
  - It should contain all the information you may need
  - The information should be found easily
  - It should be of a convenient size
  - It should be capable of expansion
  - It should be easily accessible
  - It should be stored under suitable conditions so that it won't get damaged or lose its information
- An **index** is something which makes it easier to locate information or records.
- **Cross-referencing** information is commonly carried out when items of information could be filed in more than one place, or could be needed in connection with more than one enquiry.
- The three main systems for **classifying information** are **alphabetical, numerical** and **alpha-numerical.**

## Quick quiz

1 What is a file?

2 List four systems used for arranging files.

3 What procedures might be followed when adding new information to a filing system?

4 How is information that is no longer needed on a regular basis dealt with?

5 What are classified files?

## Answers to quick quiz

1 A collection of data records with similar characteristics.

2 Alphabetical order, numerical order, alpha-numerical, chronological order.

3 Indicate that document is ready for filing, remove any paperclips and binders, place documents at random in a filing tray, determine a reference number for the document if it does not already have one, determine into which file the document is to be inserted, sort batches of documents and insert into appropriate place in appropriate files.

4
- Microfilmed or microfiched
- Archived
- Destroyed

5 Confidential or secret.

# *Answers to Activities*

## Answers to Chapter 1 activities

### Answer 1.1

(a) A balance sheet is a statement of the liabilities, capital and assets of a business at a given moment in time. It is like a 'snapshot' photograph, since it captures on paper a still image, frozen at a single moment in time, of something which is dynamic and continually changing. The balance sheet will usually show the position on the date which is the end of the **accounting period** of the business; an accounting period is usually one year.

(b) (i) **Fixed assets** are assets acquired for use within the business, rather than for selling to a customer. A fixed asset must be used by the business and it must have a 'life' in use of more than one year.

(ii) **Current assets** are:

(1) Items owned by the business with the intention of turning them into cash within one year

(2) Cash, including money in the bank, owned by the business

(c) (i) **Current liabilities** are debts of the business that must be paid within a year. This will normally include the bank overdraft as overdrafts are repayable on demand unless special terms are negotiated.

(ii) **Long-term liabilities** are debts which are not payable until some time after one year from the accounting date.

### Answer 1.2

**Revenue expenditure** results from the purchase of goods and services that will:

(a) Be used fully in the accounting period in which they are purchased, and so be a cost or expense in the profit and loss account

(b) Result in a current asset as at the end of the accounting period (because the goods or services have not yet been consumed or made use of)

**Capital expenditure** results in the purchase or improvement of fixed assets, which are assets that will provide benefits to the business in more than one accounting period, and which are not acquired to be resold in the normal course of trade. The cost of purchasing fixed assets is not charged in full to the profit and loss account of the period in which the purchase occurs. Instead, the fixed asset is gradually depreciated in the profit and loss accounts of a number of accounting periods.

Since revenue items and capital items are accounted for in different ways, the correct and consistent calculation of profit for any accounting period depends on the correct and consistent classification of items as revenue or capital.

### Answer 1.3

*Helping hand.* The profit of £14,000 in the profit and loss account should be the balancing figure in the balance sheet.

SPOCK ENTERPRISES
BALANCE SHEET AS AT 30 APRIL 20X7

| | £ | £ |
|---|---|---|
| *Fixed assets at net book value* | | |
| Freehold premises | | 87,500 |
| Fixtures and fittings | | 14,000 |
| Motor vehicles | | 15,750 |
| | | 117,250 |
| *Current assets* | | |
| Stocks | 28,000 | |
| Debtors | 875 | |
| Cash | 700 | |
| | 29,575 | |
| *Current liabilities* | | |
| Bank overdraft | 3,500 | |
| Creditors | 3,150 | |
| Tax payable | 6,125 | |
| | 12,775 | |
| *Net current assets* | | 16,800 |
| *Total assets less current liabilities* | | 134,050 |
| *Long-term liabilities* | | |
| Loan | | 43,750 |
| *Net assets* | | 90,300 |
| *Capital* | | |
| Capital as at 1 May 20X6 | | 76,300 |
| Profit for the year | | 14,000 |
| Capital as at 30 April 20X7 | | 90,300 |

SPOCK ENTERPRISES
TRADING, PROFIT AND LOSS ACCOUNT
FOR THE YEAR ENDED 30 APRIL 20X7

| | £ | £ |
|---|---|---|
| Sales | | 243,775 |
| Cost of sales | | 152,425 |
| Gross profit | | 91,350 |
| Other income | | 3,500 |
| | | 94,850 |
| Selling and distribution expenses | 25,725 | |
| Administration expenses | 25,900 | |
| Finance expenses | 29,225 | |
| | | 80,850 |
| Net profit | | 14,000 |

## Answer 1.4

You would normally expect the following documents to be involved in such a transaction.

(a) A letter of enquiry
(b) A quotation
(c) An order or letter of acceptance
(d) An order acknowledgement
(e) A delivery note
(f) An invoice
(g) A warranty or guarantee for the work performed (normally for a specified period of time)

## Answer 1.5

*Helping hand.* A trade discount is used to calculate the price at which goods change hands. In this question the price of the goods was £3,000 less a £600 trade discount, giving £2,400. The cash discount is then calculated on this figure, ie 5% of £2,400 = £120.

| | £ |
|---|---|
| 60 toasters @ £50 each | 3,000 |
| Less 20% trade discount | 600 |
| *Trade price* | 2,400 |
| Less 5% settlement discount (if taken) | 120 |
| | 2,280 |

(a) From the above, if payment is made within 14 days, the total Smith Electrical would pay is £2,280.

(b) If payment is not made within 14 days, Smith Electrical would not be able to take advantage of the cash discount and so would pay £2,400.

## Answer 1.6

(a)

**TIMEWATCH LTD**

Clock House
Chronos Road
LONDON SW3 1XZ

**INVOICE**

Invoice Number: 123456
Date 01/08/X7
Tax Point 01/08/X7
Account Number: 3365

J Smith Esq
Electromarket Ltd
112 Peters Square
Weyford
Kent CR2 2TA

Telephone Number 0171 123 4567
VAT Registration Number 457 4635 19
Northern Bank plc Code 20-25-42
Account Number 957023

| Item Code | Description | Quantity | Unit Price £ | Net Amount £ |
|---|---|---|---|---|
| 13579A | Clock radios | 25 | 10.00 | 250.00 |
| | | SALES VALUE: | | 250.00 |
| | | VAT AT 17.5%: | | 43.75 |
| | | AMOUNT PAYABLE: | | 293.75 |

Terms: payment is due within 30 days of invoice date

(b) Helping hand. The quantity, amount and dates have changed.T02W079

# TIMEWATCH LTD

Clock House
Chronos Road
LONDON SW3 1XZ

Credit Note Number: 1976

Date 15/08/X7

Tax Point 15/08/X7

Account Number: 3365

**CREDIT NOTE**

J Smith Esq
Electromarket Ltd
112 Peters Square
Weyford
Kent CR2 2TA

Telephone Number 0171 123 4567
VAT Registration Number 457 4635 19
Northern Bank plc Code 20-25-42
Account Number 957023

| Item Code | Description | Quantity | Unit Price £ | Net Amount £ |
|---|---|---|---|---|
| 13579A | Clock radios (re Inv 123456) | 5 | 10.00 | 50.00 |
| | | SALES VALUE: | | 50.00 |
| | | VAT AT 17.5%: | | 8.75 |
| | | AMOUNT OF CREDIT: | | 58.75 |

## Answers to Chapter 2 activities

### Answer 2.1

(a) Cash book
(b) Sales day book
(c) Purchase day book
(d) Cash book
(e) Sales returns day book
(f) Purchase returns day book
(g) Cash book

### Answer 2.2

(a) The two sides of the transaction are:

(i) Cash is received (**debit** cash account).
(ii) Sales increase by £60 (**credit** sales account).

CASH ACCOUNT

| | | | | | |
|---|---|---|---|---|---|
| | | £ | | | £ |
| 07.04.X7 | Sales a/c | 60 | | | |

SALES ACCOUNT

| | | | | | |
|---|---|---|---|---|---|
| | | | | | £ |
| | | | 07.04.X7 | Cash a/c | 60 |

(b) The two sides of the transaction are:

(i) Cash is paid (**credit** cash account).
(ii) Rent expense increases by £4,500 (**debit** rent account).

CASH ACCOUNT

| | | | | | |
|---|---|---|---|---|---|
| | | £ | | | £ |
| | | | 07.04.X7 | Rent a/c | 4,500 |

RENT ACCOUNT

| | | | | | |
|---|---|---|---|---|---|
| | | £ | | | £ |
| 07.04.X7 | Cash a/c | 4,500 | | | |

(c) The two sides of the transaction are:

(i) Cash is paid (**credit** cash account).
(ii) Purchases increase by £3,000 (**debit** purchases account).

CASH ACCOUNT

| | | | | | |
|---|---|---|---|---|---|
| | | £ | | | £ |
| | | | 07.04.X7 | Purchases a/c | 3,000 |

PURCHASES ACCOUNT

| | | | | | |
|---|---|---|---|---|---|
| | | £ | | | £ |
| 07.04.X7 | Cash a/c | 3,000 | | | |

(d) The two sides of the transaction are:

(i) Cash is paid (**credit** cash account).
(ii) Assets - in this case, shelves - increase by £6,000 (**debit** shelves account).

CASH ACCOUNT

| | | | | | |
|---|---|---|---|---|---|
| | | £ | | | £ |
| | | | 07.04.X7 | Shelves a/c | 6,000 |

SHELVES (ASSET) ACCOUNT

| | | £ | | | £ |
|---|---|---|---|---|---|
| 07.04.X7 | Cash a/c | 6,000 | | | |

**Tutorial note**. If all four of these transactions related to the same business, the cash account of that business would end up looking as follows.

CASH ACCOUNT

| | | £ | | | £ |
|---|---|---|---|---|---|
| 07.04.X7 | Sales a/c | 60 | 07.04.X7 | Rent a/c | 4,500 |
| | | | | Purchases a/c | 3,000 |
| | | | | Shelves a/c | 6,000 |

## Answer 2.3

| | | | | |
|---|---|---|---|---|
| (a) | DEBIT | Machine account (fixed asset) | £8,000 | |
| | CREDIT | Creditors (A) | | £8,000 |
| (b) | DEBIT | Purchases account | £500 | |
| | CREDIT | Creditors (B) | | £500 |
| (c) | DEBIT | Debtors (C) | £1,200 | |
| | CREDIT | Sales | | £1,200 |
| (d) | DEBIT | Creditors (D) | £300 | |
| | CREDIT | Cash | | £300 |
| (e) | DEBIT | Cash | £180 | |
| | CREDIT | Debtors (E) | | £180 |
| (f) | DEBIT | Wages expense | £4,000 | |
| | CREDIT | Cash | | £4,000 |
| (g) | DEBIT | Rent expense | £700 | |
| | CREDIT | Creditors (G) | | £700 |
| (h) | DEBIT | Creditors (G) | £700 | |
| | CREDIT | Cash | | £700 |
| (i) | DEBIT | Insurance expense | £90 | |
| | CREDIT | Cash | | £90 |

## Answer 2.4

| | | *Original document* | *Book of prime entry* | *Accounts in main ledger to be posted to* | |
|---|---|---|---|---|---|
| | | | | *Dr* | *Cr* |
| (a) | Sale of goods on credit | Sales invoice | Sales day book | Total debtors | Sales |
| (b) | Allowances to credit customers | Credit note | Sales returns day book | Sales/Returns inward | Total debtors |
| (c) | Daily cash takings | Till rolls and/or sales invoices and receipts, bank paying-in book | Cash book | Cash | Sales |

All these transactions would be entered into the double entry system by means of periodic postings from the books of prime entry to the main ledger.

## Answer 2.5

| | Account to be debited | Ledger | Account to be credited | Ledger |
|---|---|---|---|---|
| (a) | P Jones | Purchase | Bank | Cash book |
| (b) | Purchases | Main | Davis Wholesalers | Purchase |
| (c) | K Williams | Purchase | Returns outwards | Main |
| (d) | Fixtures | Main | Bank | Cash book |
| (e) | Fixtures | Main | Bank | Cash book |
| (f) | Purchases | Main | Cash | Cash book |
| (g) | R Newman | Sales | Sales | Main |
| (h) | Insurance | Main | Bank | Cash book |
| (i) | J Baxter | Sales | Bank | Cash book |

## Answer 2.6

(a) *Purchase of goods on credit*

(i) The supplier's invoice would be the original document.
(ii) The original entry would be made in the purchase day book.
(iii) The entries made would be:

DEBIT Purchases
CREDIT Total creditors account

assuming that a control account is part of the double entry system. If not, the entries would be:

DEBIT Purchases
CREDIT Individual supplier's account.

(b) *Allowances to credit customers on the return of faulty goods*

(i) The usual documentation is a credit note. Occasionally, however, a customer may himself issue a debit note.

(ii) The book of original entry would be the sales returns day book.

(iii) The double entry would be:

DEBIT Sales
CREDIT Total debtors control account/individual debtor's account.

(c) *Petty cash reimbursement*

(i) The original documents for the data would be receipts and a petty cash voucher.
(ii) The transaction would be entered in the petty cash book.
(iii) The double entry would be:

DEBIT Entertaining expenses
CREDIT Petty cash

## Answers to Chapter 3 activities

### Answer 3.1

*Helping hand.* You should be aware of the rounding rules when calculating VAT. However, in practical situations, particularly where sellers set a price inclusive of VAT, the calculation of VAT can be made to the nearest penny, thus ignoring the rounding rules.

(a)

| *Customer* | *Zero-rated sales* | *Standard-rated sales (gross)* | *VAT* |
|---|---|---|---|
| | £ | £ | £ |
| 1 | 72.06 | | |
| 2 | | 48.00 | 7.15 |
| 3 (1) | | 4.25 | 0.63 |
| 3 (2) | 11.70 | | |
| 4 | | –19.20 | –2.86 |
| 5 | | 92.50 | 13.78 |
| 6 | | 100.00 | 14.89 |
| 7 (1) | | 58.80 | 8.76 |
| 7 (2) | 42.97 | | |
| 8 | | 7.99 | 1.19 |
| 9 (1) | | 52.88 | 7.88 |
| 9 (2) | –8.40 | | |
| 10 | | 23.50 | 3.50 |
| | 118.33 | 368.72 | 54.92 |

Arithmetic check: $£368.72 \times \frac{17.5}{117.5} = £54.92$

The amount of VAT is £54.92. This is payable to HM Customs & Excise.

Total sales before VAT are 118.33 + (368.72 – 54.92) = £432.13.

(b)

| | | £ | £ |
|---|---|---|---|
| DEBIT | Cash account | 487.05 | |
| CREDIT | Sales account | | 432.13 |
| | Value added tax account | | 54.92 |
| | | 487.05 | 487.05 |

*Helping hand.* You might have assumed the existence of a ledger analysed in greater detail. A fuller answer is shown below.

| | | £ | £ |
|---|---|---|---|
| DEBIT | Cash account | 487.05 | |
| CREDIT | Sales - books | | 126.73 |
| | Sales - other | | 330.14 |
| DEBIT | Sales returns - books | 8.40 | |
| | Sales returns - other | 16.34 | |
| CREDIT | VAT | | 54.92 |
| | | 511.79 | 511.79 |

## Answer 3.2

(a) The relevant books of prime entry are the cash book, the sales day book and the purchase day book.

CASH BOOK (RECEIPTS)

| *Date* | *Narrative* | *Total* | *Capital* | *Sales* | *Debtors* |
|---|---|---|---|---|---|
| June | | £ | £ | £ | £ |
| 1 | Capital | 10,000 | 10,000 | | |
| 13 | Sales | 310 | | 310 | |
| 16 | Waterhouses | 1,200 | | | 1,200 |
| 24 | Books & Co | 350 | | | 350 |
| | | 11,860 | 10,000 | 310 | 1,550 |

CASH BOOK (PAYMENTS)

| *Date* | *Narrative* | *Total* | *Fixtures and fittings* | *Creditors* | *Rent* | *Delivery expenses* | *Drawings* | *Wages* |
|---|---|---|---|---|---|---|---|---|
| June | | £ | £ | £ | £ | £ | £ | £ |
| 1 | Warehouse Fittings Ltd | 3,500 | 3,500 | | | | | |
| 19 | Ransome House | 820 | | 820 | | | | |
| 20 | Rent | 300 | | | 300 | | | |
| 21 | Delivery expenses | 75 | | | | 75 | | |
| 30 | Drawings | 270 | | | | | 270 | |
| 30 | Wages | 400 | | | | | | 400 |
| 30 | Big, White | 450 | | 450 | | | | |
| | | 5,815 | 3,500 | 1,270 | 300 | 75 | 270 | 400 |

SALES DAY BOOK

| *Date* | *Customer* | *Amount* |
|---|---|---|
| June | | £ |
| 4 | Waterhouses | 1,200 |
| 11 | Books & Co | 740 |
| 18 | R S Jones | 500 |
| | | 2,440 |

PURCHASE DAY BOOK

| *Date* | *Supplier* | *Amount* |
|---|---|---|
| June | | £ |
| 2 | Ransome House | 820 |
| 9 | Big, White | 450 |
| 17 | RUP Ltd | 1,000 |
| | | 2,270 |

(b) and (c)

The relevant ledger accounts are for cash, sales, purchases, creditors, debtors, capital, fixtures and fittings, rent, delivery expenses, drawings and wages.

CASH ACCOUNT

| | £ | | £ |
|---|---|---|---|
| June receipts | 11,860 | June payments | 5,815 |
| | | Balance c/d | 6,045 |
| | 11,860 | | 11,860 |

SALES ACCOUNT

| | £ | | £ |
|---|---|---|---|
| | | Cash | 310 |
| Balance c/d | 2,750 | Debtors | 2,440 |
| | 2,750 | | 2,750 |

PURCHASES ACCOUNT

| | £ | | £ |
|---|---|---|---|
| Creditors | 2,270 | Balance c/d | 2,270 |

DEBTORS ACCOUNT

| | £ | | £ |
|---|---|---|---|
| Sales | 2,440 | Cash | 1,550 |
| | | Balance c/d | 890 |
| | 2,440 | | 2,440 |

CREDITORS ACCOUNT

| | £ | | £ |
|---|---|---|---|
| Cash | 1,270 | Purchases | 2,270 |
| Balance c/d | 1,000 | | |
| | 2,270 | | 2,270 |

CAPITAL ACCOUNT

| | £ | | |
|---|---|---|---|
| Balance c/d | 10,000 | Cash | |

FIXTURES AND FITTINGS ACCOUNT

| | £ | | £ |
|---|---|---|---|
| Cash | 3,500 | Balance c/d | 3,500 |

RENT ACCOUNT

| | £ | | |
|---|---|---|---|
| Cash | 300 | Balance c/d | 300 |

DELIVERY EXPENSES ACCOUNT

| | £ | | £ |
|---|---|---|---|
| Cash | 75 | Balance c/d | 75 |

DRAWINGS ACCOUNT

| | £ | | £ |
|---|---|---|---|
| Cash | 270 | Balance c/d | 270 |

WAGES ACCOUNT

| | £ | | £ |
|---|---|---|---|
| Cash | 400 | Balance c/d | 400 |

(d) TRIAL BALANCE AS AT 30 JUNE 20X7

| *Account* | *Dr* | *Cr* |
|---|---|---|
| | £ | £ |
| Cash | 6,045 | |
| Sales | | 2,750 |
| Purchases | 2,270 | |
| Debtors | 890 | |
| Creditors | | 1,000 |
| Capital | | 10,000 |
| Fixtures and fittings | 3,500 | |
| Rent | 300 | |
| Delivery expenses | 75 | |
| Drawings | 270 | |
| Wages | 400 | |
| | 13,750 | 13,750 |

## Answer 3.3

The main advantage of computerised accounting systems is that a large amount of data can be processed very quickly. A further advantage is that computerised systems are more accurate than manual systems.

Lou's comment that 'you never know what is going on in that funny box' might be better expressed as 'lack of audit trail'. If a mistake occurs somewhere in the system it is not always easy to identify where and how it happened.

## Answers to Chapter 4 activities

### Answer 4.1

(a) **Sheet number 72.** The bank numbers each statement sheet issued for the account. Transactions from 1 March 20X7 onwards will be shown on statement number 73, and so on. Numbering the statements in this way allows the customer to check that none of its bank statements are missing.

(b) **Bank giro credit.** The bank giro credit system enables money to be paid in to any bank for the credit of a third party's account at another bank. Pronto Motors has paid in £162.40 for the credit of Gary Jones Trading's account at Southern Bank. A bank giro credit may take around two or three days for the banks to process.

(c) **£59.03.** This shows that there is a debit balance (an overdraft) of £59.03 at the bank on 11 February 20X7. Gary Jones Trading is at that point a *debtor* of the bank; the bank is a *creditor* of Gary Jones Trading.

(d) **Direct debit.** Swingate Ltd must have authority (by means of a direct debit mandate signed on behalf of Gary Jones Trading Ltd) to make a direct debit from its account.

This arrangement allows payments to be made to a third party without a cheque having to be sent.

(e) **Bank charges.** The bank may make various charges to cover its costs in providing bank services to the customer. The bank will be able to explain how its charges are calculated.

### Answer 4.2

CASH BOOK

| *Receipts* | | | *Payments* | | |
|---|---|---|---|---|---|
| *Date* | *Details* | | *Date* | *Details* | |
| *20X7* | | £ | *20X7* | | £ |
| | Balance b/d | 596.74 | 21 Feb | Swingate | 121.00 |
| 23 Feb | Bord & Sons | 194.60 | 28 Feb | Bank charges | 15.40 |
| | | | 28 Feb | Balance c/d | 654.94 |
| | | 791.34 | | | 791.34 |

### Answer 4.3

GARY JONES TRADING LIMITED
BANK RECONCILIATION STATEMENT AS AT 28 FEBRUARY 20X7

| | £ | £ |
|---|---|---|
| Balance per bank statement | | 611.93 |
| Add outstanding lodgement (Warleys Ltd) | | 342.50 |
| | | 954.43 |
| Less: unpresented cheques | | |
| 800124 | 207.05 | |
| 800125 | 92.44 | |
| | | (299.49) |
| Balance per cash book | | 654.94 |

### Answer 4.4

(a) (i) CASH BOOK

| | £ | | £ |
|---|---|---|---|
| Uncorrected balance b/d | 24.13 | Overdraft interest | 24.88 |
| Error in cash book | 27.00 | Balance c/d | 26.25 |
| | 51.13 | | 51.13 |

(ii) GEMFIX ENGINEERING LIMITED
BANK RECONCILIATION STATEMENT AS AT 31 OCTOBER 20X7

| | £ |
|---|---|
| Balance as per bank statement (overdrawn) | (142.50) |
| Less unpresented cheques (total) | (121.25) |
| | (263.75) |
| Add cheque paid in, not yet credited on bank statement | 290.00 |
| Balance as per cash book | 26.25 |

(b) There are three reasons why bank reconciliation statements should be prepared regularly and on time.

(i) The company's records should be updated for items such as bank charges and dishonoured cheques so that managers are not working with an incorrect figure for the bank balance.

(ii) Errors should be identified and corrected as soon as possible, whether they are made by the company or by the bank.

(iii) Checks should be made on the time delay between cheques being written and their presentation for payment, and to check the time taken for cheques and cash paid in to be credited to the account. A better understanding of such timing differences will help managers to improve their cash planning.

## Answer 4.5

**CASH BOOK**

| Date 20X0 | Details | Bank £ | Date 20X0 | Cheque No | Details | Bank £ |
|---|---|---|---|---|---|---|
| 1 Sept | Balance b/f | 13,400 | 1 Sept | 108300 | J Hibbert | 1,200 |
| 1 Sept | L Peters | 400 | 5 Sept | 108301 | Cleanglass | 470 |
| 28 Sept | John Smith | 2,400 | 25 Sept | 108302 | Denham Insurers | 630 |
| 29 Sept | KKG Ltd | 144 | 29 Sept | 108303 | Kelvin Ltd | 160 |
| 8 Sept | Zebra Sales | 4,000 | | | Salaries | 9,024 |
| 30 Sept | Bristol Ltd | 2,000 | | | West Council | 300 |
| | | | | | Any Bank | 400 |
| | | | | | Bank charges | 132 |
| | | | | | Balance c/d | 10,028 |
| | | 22,344 | | | | 22,344 |
| | Balance b/d | 10,028 | | | | |

**Reasons why the Cash Book Balance differs from the Bank Statement**

1 Uncleared receipt from John Smith: £2,400

2 Uncleared receipt from KKG Ltd: £144

3 Unpresented cheque to Denham Insurers: £630

**Tutorial note**

We can prove this, although you wouldn't need to in a central assessment.

| | £ |
|---|---|
| Balance per bank statement | 8,114 |
| Less unpresented cheque | (630) |
| | 7,484 |
| Add uncleared receipts (2,400 + 144) | 2,544 |
| Balance per cash book | 10,028 |

## Answers to Chapter 5 activities

### Answer 5.1

**STOCK RECORD CARD – SB 248 RAPIDTAN SUNBEDS**

| Date 20X0 | Details | In | Out | Quantity in stock | @ £500 per sunbed £ |
|---|---|---|---|---|---|
| 1 Jan | Opening balance | | | 174 | 87,000 |
| 1 Jan | Sales | | 10 | 164 | 82,000 |
| 4 Jan | Sales | | 20 | 144 | 72,000 |
| 6 Jan | Sales | | 50 | 94 | 47,000 |
| 7 Jan | Sales | | 15 | 79 | 39,500 |
| 11 Jan | Sales | | 20 | 59 | 29,500 |
| 12 Jan | Faulty | | 1 | 58 | 29,000 |
| 13 Jan | Sales | | 20 | 38 | 19,000 |
| 15 Jan | Sales | | 20 | 18 | 9,000 |
| 18 Jan | Receipt | 100 | | 118 | 59,000 |
| 20 Jan | Sales | | 10 | 108 | 54,000 |
| 22 Jan | Sales | | 5 | 103 | 51,500 |
| 25 Jan | Sales | | 15 | 88 | 44,000 |
| 26 Jan | Sales | | 20 | 68 | 34,000 |
| 28 Jan | Receipt | 110 | | 178 | 89,000 |
| 29 Jan | Sales | | 20 | 158 | 79,000 |
| 30 Jan | Sales | | 20 | 138 | 69,000 |

**RECONCILIATION OF STOCK RECORD WITH PHYSICAL STOCK CHECK ON 31 JANUARY 20X0**

| | |
|---|---|
| PHYSICAL STOCK CHECK 139 @ £500 | 69,500 |
| STORES RECORD CARD QUANTITY | 69,000 |
| DIFFERENCE | £500 |

**NOTE FOR SUPERVISOR**

There is a difference of £500 between the value of item SB 248 as reported in the physical stock check and the value on the stores card.

The probable reason for this is the item shown as faulty on 12 January. This may have been included in the stock check by mistake.

## Answer 5.2

WAGES CONTROL

| Date 20X1 | Details | £ | Date 20X1 | Details | £ |
|---|---|---|---|---|---|
| 30 June | Net wages | 6,140 | 30 June | Gross wages | 8,600 |
| 30 June | Employer's NIC | 1,000 | 30 June | Employer's NIC | 1,000 |
| 30 June | Employees' NIC | 820 | | | |
| 30 June | Trade Union fees | 140 | | | |
| 30 June | PAYE | 1,500 | | | |
| | | 9,600 | | | 9,600 |

## Answer 5.3

PETTY CASH CONTROL

| Date 20X1 | Details | £ | Date 20X1 | Details | £ |
|---|---|---|---|---|---|
| 1 Aug | Balance b/f | 214 | 31 Aug | Petty cash | 196 |
| 31 Aug | Bank | 200 | 31 Aug | Balance c/d | 218 |
| | | 414 | | | 414 |
| 1 Sept | Balance b/d | 218 | | | |

## Answer 5.4

DEBTORS ACCOUNT

| | | £ | | | £ |
|---|---|---|---|---|---|
| 1.10.X1 | Balance b/f (b) | 30,000 | 15.1.X2 | Bad debts-Fall Ltd (c) | 2,000 |
| 30.9.X2 | Sales (d) | 187,800 | 30.9.X2 | Cash (e) | 182,500 |
| | | | | Discounts allowed (f) | 5,300 |
| | | | | Bad debts (g) | 3,500 |
| | | | | Balance c/d | 24,500 |
| | | 217,800 | | | 217,800 |
| 1.10.X2 | Balance b/d | 24,500 | | | |

SALES ACCOUNT

| | | £ | | | £ |
|---|---|---|---|---|---|
| 30.9.X2 | Trading P & L a/c | 234,600 | 30.9.X2 | Cash (d) | 46,800 |
| | | | | Debtors (d) | 187,800 |
| | | 234,600 | | | 234,600 |

BAD DEBTS ACCOUNT

| | | £ | | | £ |
|---|---|---|---|---|---|
| 15.1.X2 | Debtors-Fall Ltd (c) | 2,000 | 30.9.X2 | Trading P & L a/c | 5,500 |
| 30.9.X2 | Debtors (g) | 3,500 | | | |
| | | 5,500 | | | 5,500 |

PROVISION FOR DOUBTFUL DEBTS ACCOUNT

| | | £ | | | £ |
|---|---|---|---|---|---|
| 30.9.X2 | Balance c/d (h) | | 1.10.X1 | Balance b/f (b) | |
| | 5% × £24,500 | 1,225 | | 5% × £30,000 | 1,500 |
| | Trading P & L a/c - reduction in provision | 275 | | | |
| | | 1,500 | | | 1,500 |
| | | | 1.10.X2 | Balance b/d | 1,225 |

*Helping hand.* Settlement discounts go on the credit side of the debtors account, like cash.

DISCOUNTS ALLOWED ACCOUNT

| | | £ | | | £ |
|---|---|---|---|---|---|
| 30.9.X2 | Debtors | 5,300 | 30.9.X2 | Trading P & L a/c | 5,300 |

CASH ACCOUNT (EXTRACT)

| | | £ |
|---|---|---|
| 30.9.X2 | Debtors | 182,500 |
| | Sales | 46,800 |

TRADING PROFIT AND LOSS ACCOUNT (EXTRACT)

| | | £ | | | £ |
|---|---|---|---|---|---|
| 30.9.X2 | Bad debts | 5,500 | 30.9.X2 | Sales | 234,600 |
| | Discounts allowed | 5,300 | | Provision for doubtful debts | 275 |

# Answers to Chapter 6 activities

## Answer 6.1

SALES LEDGER CONTROL ACCOUNT

| | | £ | | | £ |
|---|---|---|---|---|---|
| Debit balances b/d | (1) | X | Credit balances b/d | (1) | X |
| Sales | (2) | X | Cash receipts | (3) | X |
| Bank (refunds) | (3) or (5) | X | Credit notes | (4) | X |
| Bank (dishonoured cheques) | (3) or (5) | X | Bad debt expense | (5) | X |
| Credit balances c/d | (6) | X | Discount allowed* | (3) | X |
| | | | Debit balances c/d | (6) | X |
| | | X | | | X |

Sources of entries

(1) Brought down from previous period's control account once closed off.
(2) Sales day book.
(3) Cash book and petty cash book.
(4) Sales returns day book.
(5) Journal.
(6) Calculated and reconciled with sales ledger total of balances.

*Helping hand*

* Discounts allowed reflects only cash or settlement discounts, not trade discounts.

** Individual entries to the account would be dated and would have folio references to the appropriate book of prime entry/journal. These details have been omitted for the purposes of clarity.

## Answer 6.2

ITEMS NOT APPEARING IN THE SALES LEDGER CONTROL ACCOUNT

*1 and 2 Credit and debit balances on individual debtor account*

*Individual* debtors accounts do not appear in the sales ledger control account, although the transactions which give rise to them (sales, cash receipts etc) do. The sales ledger control account is a total account.

*3 Cash sales*

The sales ledger control account deals with sales made on credit. Cash sales (*Debit* Cash; *Credit* Sales) have nothing to do with it.

*5 Provision for bad and doubtful debts*

This is a *separate account* from the sales ledger control account, even though it has the overall effect of reducing the value of the assets represented by the sales ledger control account.

*7 Trade discounts received*

These are discounts on what has been purchased, so have nothing to do with sales.

*11 Credit notes received*

These have the effect of reducing what *we* owe to other people, so they have nothing to do with the sales ledger control account.

ITEMS THAT DO APPEAR IN THE SALES LEDGER CONTROL ACCOUNT

*4 Sales on credit*

This should need no explaining.

*6 Settlement discounts allowed*

A settlement discount is given to a debtor who pays early, and so reduces the value of the debt. So if someone owes £100, but you say that you'll reduce the amount to £95 if they pay within 2 weeks, then they have received, and you have given, a settlement discount of £5. The whole of the original debt is cleared - of the £100 owed, your customer has paid £95, and you have basically written off £5 to the profit and loss account.

*8 Cash receipts*

These are payments from debtors. They reduce the debt.

*9 Bad debts written off*

Writing off a bad debt involves removing the debt from the sales ledger and making a corresponding entry to the sales ledger control account, and then the profit and loss account.

*10 Sales returns*

These arise when sold goods are returned and the return is accepted. The debtor no longer owes the money, so the debt is cancelled. Sales returns would be posted from the sales returns day book as a total, a method similar to the way in which total sales are posted from the sales day book.

*12 Credit notes issued*

A credit note can be issued to reduce the value of the debt. This might be the result of a sales return, or correction of an error. (Note that if separate records of sales returns are processed, credit notes would only be processed in respect of other items, so as to avoid any double counting.)

## Answer 6.3

(a) UNADJUSTED SALES LEDGER CONTROL ACCOUNT

| | £ | | £ |
|---|---|---|---|
| Balance b/d | 12,404.86 | Balance b/d | 322.94 |
| Sales | 96,464.41 | Returns inwards | 1,142.92 |
| Bank: cheques dishonoured | 192.00 | Bank | 94,648.71 |
| Balance c/d | 337.75 | Discounts allowed | 3,311.47 |
| | | Balance c/d | 9,972.98 |
| | 109,399.02 | | 109,399.02 |
| Balance b/d | 9,972.98 | Balance b/d | 337.75 |

(b) ADJUSTED SALES LEDGER CONTROL ACCOUNT

| | £ | | £ |
|---|---|---|---|
| Unadjusted balance b/d | 9,972.98 | Unadjusted balance b/d | 337.75 |
| Sales: receipts from cash sales wrongly credited to debtors | 3,440.00 | Bad debt written off | 77.00 |
| Sales day book undercast | 427.80 | Returns outwards: returns to suppliers wrongly debited to debtors | 3,711.86 |
| Balance c/d | 337.75 | Balance c/d | 10,051.92 |
| | 14,178.53 | | 14,178.53 |
| Balance b/d | 10,051.92 | Balance b/d | 337.75 |

Supernova Ltd has debtors of £10,051.92. It also has a creditor of £337.75.

Errors (v ) and (vi) relate to entries in individual customer accounts in the sales ledger and have no effect on the control account in the general ledger.

## Answer 6.4

(a)

SALES LEDGER CONTROL

| | | £ | | | £ |
|---|---|---|---|---|---|
| 1.12.X6 | Balance b/d | 50,241 | 20X7 | Returns inwards | 41,226 |
| 20X7 | Sales | 472,185 | | Bad debts written off | 1,914 |
| | Cheques dishonoured | 626 | | Discounts allowed | 2,672 |
| | | | | Cheques received | 429,811 |
| | | | 30.11 | Balance c/d | 47,429 |
| | | 523,052 | | | 523,052 |

(b)

| | £ | £ |
|---|---|---|
| Balance per P Johnson | | 46,347 |
| Add: Whitchurch Ltd invoice, previously omitted from ledger | 267 | |
| Rectofen Ltd balance, previously omitted from list | 2,435 | |
| Casting error in list total (£46,747, not £46,347) | 400 | |
| | | 3,102 |
| | | 49,449 |
| Less: Error on posting of Bury plc's credit note to ledger | 20 | |
| P Fox & Son (Swindon) td's balance included twice | 2,000 | |
| | | 2,020 |
| Balance per sales ledger control account | | 47,429 |

## Answers to Chapter 7 activities

### Answer 7.1

Answer C is correct.

*Helping hand.* Computerisation has meant that a number of different ways of processing creditors can be implemented. Some of these you might encounter in your work. Two examples are given below.

(a) A separate purchase ledger module is *not* maintained. There is no purchase ledger control account. Instead there is a separate account for every creditor in the general ledger.

(b) A separate purchase ledger module is maintained, but the role of the purchase day book is different in that each invoice is posted individually to the purchase ledger control account, VAT account, and purchase ledger account (ie the posting to the purchase ledger control account is not on a summary basis). The control account is still only a total account, however.

The use of the purchase day book and the purchase ledger, as separate from the general ledger to which summary postings are made, is merely for *convenience*.

### Answer 7.2

FALSE

In any accounting system, whether computerised or manual, accounts can be altered by use of the journal. It would be quite possible to make adjustments to the purchase ledger control account which, for whatever reason, are not reflected in the purchase ledger. So, while the purchase ledger updates the purchase ledger control account, there might be other differences.

It depends on which type of accounting system is used.

### Answer 7.3

(a) All of them.

(i) Not all cash payments are to trade creditors so a payment could be given a wrong nominal ledger account code.

(ii) These could be found in a manual system, or could be caused by a fault in a computer program.

(iii) Transposition errors could be caused if the purchase ledger, nominal ledger and purchase day book were separate, and there were manual postings.

(b) (i) Dividend payments and (iii) drawings do not relate in any way to trade creditors.

(c) FALSE. You might overpay a supplier, or pay before the goods have been received and invoiced, or pay the wrong supplier.

### Answer 7.4

WALLACE AND GROMMET
RECONCILIATION OF PURCHASE LEDGER BALANCES WITH THE PURCHASE LEDGER CONTROL ACCOUNT AS AT 31 JULY 20X7

| | | £ | £ |
|---|---|---|---|
| (a) | Balances according to purchase ledger | | 54,842.40 |
| | Add: Account omitted | 8,300.00 | |
| | RNH's account undercast | 620.40 | |
| | | | 8,920.40 |
| | | | 63,762.80 |
| | Deduct: Cheque not debited to SPL's account | 5,000.00 | |
| | Contra arrangement omitted | 400.00 | |
| | | | 5,400.00 |
| | Amended balance as at 31 July 20X7 | | 58,362.80 |

*Helping hand.* The cheque for £5,000 is deducted. If it had been properly debited in the first place it would have **reduced** SPL's balance.

| | | £ | £ |
|---|---|---|---|
| (b) | Balance according to the purchase ledger control account | | 57,997.34 |
| | Add: Discounts received entered twice | 740.36 | |
| | Purchase for June | 7,449.60 | |
| | | | 8,189.96 |
| | | | 66,187.30 |
| | Deduct: Vehicle erroneously entered as purchases | 6,400.00 | |
| | Returns outward omitted from account | 1,424.50 | |
| | | | 7,824.50 |
| | Amended balance as at 31 July 20X7 | | 58,362.80 |

## Answers to Chapter 8 activities

### Answer 8.1

You should have noted the following details.

| | |
|---|---|
| Our (Lightfoot & Co's) reference: | Z/0335/MJD |
| Department: | Purchasing |
| Supplier name: | Sandimans Ltd |
| Previous correspondence: | 11 April 20X6 |
| Present correspondence: | 4 May 20X6 |
| Subject: | Stationery (invoice 147829) |

It is most unlikely that details like the geographical source of the letter or the name of its writer would be needed for filing purposes.

The accounts department should be sent a copy so that they can chase up the cheque that has not been received.

### Answer 8.2

(a) The order would be: 15, 21, 28, 2, 8, 1, 18 and 26, 16, 13, 3, 12, 22, 30, 27, 4, 5, 9, 19, 25, 6, 29, 23, 24, 20, 17, 7, 10, 14, 11.

*Helping hand.* A good approach would have been to highlight all the documents of the same year in the same colour, thereby breaking down the task into more manageable portions.

(b) 54321 Discos (7)
Argent-Smith M (11)
Argentson S (21)
Bexley J (5)
Bidwell D (4)
Briton N (28)
Britton T (12)
BRJ Plumbing (19)
Cottrell J (1)
Crown Dr J (8)
Emly P (17)
Gisling B (20)
Harrison P (27)
Harry Holden Ltd (18)
Holden R (2)
ILD Services Ltd (23)
Kelsey L C (22)
Locke D (9)
McLaughlin D (13)
Maclean T (6)
O'Grady E (15)
Page W (26)
Richmond A (29)
Saint Francis Pet Shop (16)
Sainton E (10)
St Olave's Church (30)
Van Saintby A (24)
Williams J (3)
Williams J A (14)
Williams John (25)

*Helping hand.* Slight variations are possible, for example with the treatment of numbers and initials, depending upon the policy of the organisation.

(c) The order would be: 3, 18, 27, 23, 19, 13, 10, 7, 15, 30, 26, 5, 21, 24, 6.

(d) Geographical classification by towns gives the following results.

| | |
|---|---|
| Bexley: | 2, 7, 11, 18, 28 |
| Bromley: | 1, 10, 22, 24, 30 |
| Crayford: | 9, 12, 19, 26, 29 |
| Dartford: | 3, 4, 16, 21, 25, 27 |
| Orpington: | 5, 6, 13, 17, 23 |
| Sidcup: | 15 |
| Woolwich: | 8, 14, 20 |

## Answer 8.3

You were asked for relevant examples from your own workplace.

## Answer 8.4

(a) There is room for some flexibility in answers here - what follows is very much a suggestion.

1 The bill is not confidential if Mr Glover chooses not to keep it so. It is nothing to do with your organisation anyway.

2 Not confidential. The reference that was given might be, but this is not mentioned.

3 This is probably very confidential: public knowledge of merger proposals could affect the outcome of the negotiations.

4 This may or may not be confidential depending upon your own organisation's policy. The general view is that budgeting should be done with the involvement of staff, so we are inclined to say that this is not, on the face of it, a confidential document.

5 This is obviously a highly personal document: it should be filed away in your personnel file.

6 This is probably not confidential. The familiarity of the signature is most likely to be due to the length of time your manager and 'Nancy' have been dealing with each other. If not, your manager is not ashamed of it and what business is it of yours anyway?

7 There is nothing confidential about this: the surname is irrelevant.

8 Mrs Paribus's letter is probably not particularly confidential although the nature of her complaint might make it so. To preserve the reputation of your organisation it might be better to shut it away in a file to stop cleaners, caterers or other external parties reading it.

9 This material is published: it is clearly not confidential.

10 There is no reason why personal details of directors should be confidential. If the list or an item on it had a heading or note such as 'Do not disclose to anyone below the level of Senior Manager', however, your manager should be ensuring that it does not fall into the wrong hands.

To summarise, documents 3 and 5 are definitely confidential, and documents 2, 7 and 9 are definitely not. The remainder may or may not be confidential depending on the circumstances, and whose point of view you are considering the matter from.

(b) The danger here is that your fax will be collected by someone other than your manager. Its contents seem as if they might be damaging to your organisation in the wrong hands. You should therefore ring your manager and discuss the problem with him. The best solution is probably for him to stand over the receiving fax machine until your fax is received.

# *List of key terms and index*

## ORDER FORM

Any books from our AAT range can be ordered by telephoning 020 8740 2211. Alternatively, send this page to our address below, fax it to us on 020 8740 1184, or email us at **publishing@bpp.com.** Or order from our website: www.bpp.com

We aim to deliver to all UK addresses inside 5 working days; a signature will be required. Orders to all EU addresses should be delivered within 6 working days. All other orders to overseas addresses should be delivered within 8 working days.

**To: BPP Publishing Ltd, Aldine House, Aldine Place, London W12 8AW**

**Tel: 020-8740 2211 Fax: 020-8740 1184 Email:** publishing@bpp.com **Website:** www.bpp.com

Mr / Ms (full name): ______________________________

Daytime delivery address: ______________________________

______________________________

Postcode: ____________________ Daytime Tel: ______________________________

Please send me the following quantities of books.

| | *5/01 Interactive Text* | *8/01 DA Kit* | *8/01 Combined Kit* | *8/01 CA Kit* |
|---|---|---|---|---|
| **FOUNDATION** | | | | |
| Unit 1 Recording Income and Receipts (6/01 Kit) | ☐ | ☐ | | |
| Unit 2 Making and Recording Payments (6/01 Kit) | ☐ | ☐ | | |
| Unit 3 Ledger Balances and Initial Trial Balance (6/01 Kit) | ☐ | | ☐ | |
| Unit 4 Supplying Information for Management Control (6/01 Kit) | ☐ | ☐ | | |
| Unit 20 Working with Information Technology (8/01 Text) | ☐ | | | |
| Unit 22/23 Healthy Workplace and Personal Effectiveness | ☐ | | | |
| **INTERMEDIATE** | | | | |
| Unit 5 Financial Records and Accounts | ☐ | | ☐ | |
| Unit 6 Cost Information | ☐ | | ☐ | |
| Unit 7 Reports and Returns | ☐ | ☐ | | |
| Unit 21 Using Information Technology | ☐ | ☐ | | |
| **TECHNICIAN** | | | | |
| Unit 8/9 Core Managing Costs and Allocating Resources | ☐ | | | ☐ |
| Unit 10 Core Managing Accounting Systems | ☐ | ☐ | | |
| Unit 11 Option Financial Statements (Accounting Practice) | ☐ | | | ☐ |
| Unit 12 Option Financial Statements (Central Government) | ☐ | | | ☐ |
| Unit 15 Option Cash Management and Credit Control | ☐ | ☐ | | |
| Unit 16 Option Evaluating Activities | ☐ | ☐ | | |
| Unit 17 Option Implementing Auditing Procedures | ☐ | ☐ | | |
| Unit 18 Option Business Tax FA01(8/01 Text) | ☐ | ☐ | | |
| Unit 19 Option Personal Tax FA01(8/01 Text) | ☐ | ☐ | | |
| **TECHNICIAN 2000** | | | | |
| Unit 18 Option Business Tax FA00 (8/00 Text & Kit) | ☐ | ☐ | | |
| Unit 19 Option Personal Tax FA00 (8/00 Text & Kit) | ☐ | ☐ | | |

TOTAL BOOKS ☐ + ☐ + ☐ + ☐ = ☐

| | |
|---|---|
| **Special offer** @ £9.95 each = | £ |
| Foundation units £80 Complete set of 10 books | £ |
| Intermediate units £65 Complete set of 8 books | £ |
| Technician units £100 Set of 12 books (please specify above which titles you require) | £ |

**Postage and packaging**

**UK:** £2.00 for each book to maximum of £10

**Europe (inc ROI and Channel Islands):** £4.00 for first book, £2.00 for each extra

**Rest of the World:** £20.00 for first book, £10 for each extra

P & P £

**GRAND TOTAL** £

**I enclose a cheque for £ _________ (cheques to BPP Publishing Ltd) or charge to Mastercard/Visa/Switch**

**Card number** ☐☐☐☐☐☐☐☐☐☐☐☐☐☐☐☐☐☐

**Start date** ____________________ **Expiry date** ________________ **Issue no. (Switch only)**______

**Signature** ______________________________

## REVIEW FORM & FREE PRIZE DRAW

All original review forms from the entire BPP range, completed with genuine comments, will be entered into one of two draws on 31 January 2002 and 31 July 2002. The names on the first four forms picked out on each occasion will be sent a cheque for £50.

**Name:** ______________________ **Address:** ______________________

______________________

______________________

**How have you used this Interactive Text?**
*(Tick one box only)*

☐ Home study (book only)

☐ On a course: college ______________

☐ With 'correspondence' package

☐ Other ______________

**Why did you decide to purchase this Interactive Text?** *(Tick one box only)*

☐ Have used BPP Texts in the past

☐ Recommendation by friend/colleague

☐ Recommendation by a lecturer at college

☐ Saw advertising

☐ Other ______________

**During the past six months do you recall seeing/receiving any of the following?**
*(Tick as many boxes as are relevant)*

☐ Our advertisement in *Accounting Technician* magazine

☐ Our advertisement in *Pass*

☐ Our brochure with a letter through the post

**Which (if any) aspects of our advertising do you find useful?**
*(Tick as many boxes as are relevant)*

☐ Prices and publication dates of new editions

☐ Information on Interactive Text content

☐ Facility to order books off-the-page

☐ None of the above

**Have you used the companion Assessment Kit for this subject?** ☐ **Yes** ☐ **No**

**Your ratings, comments and suggestions would be appreciated on the following areas**

| | *Very useful* | *Useful* | *Not useful* |
|---|---|---|---|
| *Introductory section (How to use this Interactive Text etc)* | ☐ | ☐ | ☐ |
| *Chapter topic lists* | ☐ | ☐ | ☐ |
| *Chapter learning objectives* | ☐ | ☐ | ☐ |
| *Key terms* | ☐ | ☐ | ☐ |
| *Assessment alerts* | ☐ | ☐ | ☐ |
| *Examples* | ☐ | ☐ | ☐ |
| *Activities and answers* | ☐ | ☐ | ☐ |
| *Key learning points* | ☐ | ☐ | ☐ |
| *Quick quizzes and answers* | ☐ | ☐ | ☐ |
| *List of key terms and index* | ☐ | ☐ | ☐ |
| *Icons* | ☐ | ☐ | ☐ |

| | *Excellent* | *Good* | *Adequate* | *Poor* |
|---|---|---|---|---|
| *Overall opinion of this Text* | ☐ | ☐ | ☐ | ☐ |

**Do you intend to continue using BPP Interactive Texts/Assessment Kits?** ☐ Yes ☐ No

**Please note any further comments and suggestions/errors on the reverse of this page.**

**Please return to: Nick Weller, BPP Publishing Ltd, FREEPOST, London, W12 8BR**

## REVIEW FORM & FREE PRIZE DRAW (continued)

**Please note any further comments and suggestions/errors below**

### FREE PRIZE DRAW RULES

1 Closing date for 31 January 2002 draw is 31 December 2001. Closing date for 31 July 2002 draw is 30 June 2002.

2 Restricted to entries with UK and Eire addresses only. BPP employees, their families and business associates are excluded.

3 No purchase necessary. Entry forms are available upon request from BPP Publishing. No more than one entry per title, per person. Draw restricted to persons aged 16 and over.

4 Winners will be notified by post and receive their cheques not later than 6 weeks after the relevant draw date.

5 The decision of the promoter in all matters is final and binding. No correspondence will be entered into.